# I Want to Bear Fruit

**YOU CAN LEARN TO REACH LOST PEOPLE WITHOUT PRESSURING OTHERS OR EMBARRASSING YOURSELF**

D0062572

## CHUCK QUINLEY

Library of Congress Catalog Card Number:

ISBN: 0-87148-140-5


Copyright © 2000 by Chuck Quinley
1130 Ponderosa Drive NW
Cleveland, TN 30340
USA

Additional copies of this book can be ordered from:
Mt. Paran Bookstore
2055 Mt. Paran Rd NW
Atlanta, GA 30327
Phone:  (404) 261-0720 ext. 231
Fax:  (404) 233-6335
Email:  bookstore@mtparan.org

Chuck and Sherry Quinley can be contacted at chuck@quinley.com and sherry@quinley.com. Please visit the CQ Island Ministries website at:
www.quinley.com
for more informaion on the ministry of Chuck and Sherry and for details on sponsoring their missions work in Asia.

Those interested in contacting Towie Vasquez for graphic design services can find him at: towzter@hotmail.com. For page layout design, contact Purita dela Cruz at: pm_delacruz@yahoo.com.

# Dedication

*T*his book is affectionately dedicated to Jim and Helen Mann, the first people to ever demonstrate to me what it means to love the lost every day. In my early Christian walk, I visited and traveled with them from Atlanta to Mexico. In amazement, I watched their anointed touch on the life of every waitress and gas station attendant they encountered. No one was ever the same after meeting them. Entering their ministry as two lay people in their mid-50's, they accomplished more for God than any pastors I have ever known. Over 130 churches exist today because of them.

Upon marrying Sherry, one of my first orders of business was to take her to meet Jim and Helen before Jim went on to his reward. After Jim's death, Helen continued in her ministry to Mexico and saw over 70 more churches planted and constructed. She is in her 80's now, and continues to fight the limitations of her body so that she can touch more lives. Thank you, Jim and Helen, for giving us a model of practical, common sense spirituality as a pattern for our lives. Only heaven will reveal the true fruitfulness of your devoted lives.

We Love You!!!

CHUCK AND SHERRY

# Contents

# Foreword

*H*aving been involved in world missions at the local church level, it came as no surprise to many that in the mid 90's my wife, Susan, our second daughter, Jessica, and I found ourselves in Asia serving as missionaries. My family had been saying for years that, each time I came home from yet another overseas missions adventure, only part of me had returned.

God was drawing us to the foreign missions fields to teach us many things about Him and His ways, but mostly about ourselves. One of my greatest lessons would be to learn the vast difference between having been a missions pastor responsible for many missionaries, to now being one of those missionaries in need of a loving and supporting missions pastor.

We thought that God might have been preparing us for service in Brazil, Jamaica or even Siberia, Russia. But the one place that had never been considered was the Republic of the Philippines. Almost 9000 miles from home. Twelve time zones away. Twenty hours by air on a jumbo jet. Yet, this would become the nation and the people who would soon win our hearts, change our view of world missions and our paradigm for reaching lost people.

We served in the Philippines for a relatively short span, just over two years. However, these years have brought more change in us than any period before or since. And, in hindsight, they served as groundbreaking preparation years for the ministry that God now has us overseeing here in the US.

Chuck and Sherry Quinley have been close personal friends, as well as a source of enviable inspiration for many years.

Never did we imagine that our paths would come together for a season of ministry in one of the most exciting harvest fields that the Church has seen thus far—the heart of what has become known as the 10/40 Window.

When Susan and I first visited in late spring of 1994 for a two-week "fact finding" trip, we discovered a church of just over 300 people meeting in a large, specially designed church house for a vibrant Sunday morning worship service. What a day this was! We had arrived just a couple of days prior, and already we knew that this was where our futures would be found.

The people were warm, genuine and seemed immediately like never-before-met family members. The leadership style of the Quinleys was contagious. In the following days, the more we sat and listened to Chuck's depth of teaching, the more we could hardly wait to be there full time. He had a way of making us think about old things in a new way.

From that day to this, our admiration for the lives of Chuck and Sherry Quinley has never diminished. They practice what they preach. Equally, we continue to be challenged by the insight and wisdom of Chuck's teaching. He is gifted in taking biblical concepts and making them "daily livable."

Don't be fooled by the simplicity of this book. These pages are profound. Their principles have been tried and tested in the crucible of the daily lives of this remarkable couple. If you can but somehow catch the vision of these practical, yet powerful guidelines for friendship evangelism, you will be amazed at how easy it becomes to impact lives for the cause of Christ. No more excuses!

TERRY ROSS
Director of World Missions
Grace Fellowship

# Acknowledgements

*I* wish to convey my deepest appreciation for the many people whose help was essential in the publication of this book.

*To the Amazingly gifted Filipino staff who put the material in publishing form:*

- TOWIE VASQUEZ, an artistic genius, for the illustrations and cover art. You really made the difference in how people will initially judge the book.
- PURITA DE LA CRUZ, for her expertise in layout and formatting. You are a true professional and a friend. Thanks for working under tight constraints and for your burden to see Filipino people come to Christ.
- TOSCA PACIS, for her editing skill, rearranging so many mistakes. Thanks for your diligence and willingness to work under pressure while you had many other things going, personally.
- SARITA LADIOS, my loyal secretary, for shielding me and handling my personal stuff so I could focus on writing.

*To the American team:*

- SUSAN ROSS, for your diligent proofreading and editing, working by email half-way around the world, so we could get things done on time. Thanks for working even while nursing yourself and Terry back to health. TERRY ROSS, thanks for your friendship and encouragement.

*To My Family:*

- SHERRY, for walking through life with me for the last 20 years, and for having such a great attitude in dealing with missionary life. Aside from Christ, you are the greatest thing that has ever happened to me.

– To our six wonderful, practically-perfect children: ANDREW, KRISTIN, NATHAN, JESSICA, BROOKE, and JULIA, for understanding the value of people and never complaining when we spend time entertaining others in order to lead them to Christ. You have carried the load of this ministry along with us, and your Mom and I love you so much for your cooperation in everything the Lord has called us into.

– To our parents, WARREN and DOROTHY QUINLEY and SAM and AUDREY SMITH, for raising us with a godly fear and for accepting the sacrifice of releasing us to obey God's call into missions.

– To the MANDEVILLE NEW TESTAMENT CHURCH OF GOD and to BRO. and SIS. REID, for the lessons you taught us about serving the Lord and for accepting us when we were so young and untested in pastoring. We are strong today because of you. Keep praying!

– To our LIGHTHOUSE CHRISTIAN COMMUNITY family, who adopted us so many years ago and who have been our family for the last fifteen years. May God reward each of you for loving strangers!

# Introduction

*"This is to my Father's glory, that you bear much
fruit, showing yourselves to be my disciples...You
did not choose me, but I chose you and appointed
you to go and bear fruit—fruit that will last. . . ."*
(John 15.8, 16 NIV)

*I*n these verses, Jesus said that the way to bring glory
to the Father and to show that you are truly his disciple is to bear much fruit. I want to bear fruit. God
knows my heart. All I want in this life is to bear fruit unto
Him. I don't have to be known. I don't have to be rich. I
just want to bear fruit as the closing moments of our
planet's history tick down to zero. I imagine that you are
reading this book out of the same desire.

Thankfully, bearing fruit is actually easy to do if you are
a disciple of Christ. Read the second verse above. Christ
chose us and appointed us just for the purpose of fruit
bearing. We are made for it, whether we realize it or
not. Sixteen years ago, I was a barren Christian. I had
never led anyone to the Lord. I felt pressure and condem-
nation. My few early efforts to evangelize failed miser-
ably. Then, through the events recounted in these pages,
Sherry and I learned how spiritual harvesting works.
We want to share this with you so that your joy may be
full also.

If you want to know what to do with your life, or where to
find meaning it's simple: bear fruit! That's all there is. Be a
plumber or a painter or a pastor (whatever you are suited
and called for) but the important thing is to bear fruit.
Anything that increases our fruitfulness is good, pursue it.

Anything that gets in the way of our being fruitful, even if it pays well, is a bad thing. Leave it. That's how disciples make choices in life. They simply ask, "What will help me bear more fruit?"

In this book I won't explain how to be saved. There are many great tracts, etc., on that vital subject. I am more concerned about teaching you how to get into a relational position to share the gospel with friends and even with strangers.

As we travel the globe, Sherry and I have become particularly concerned for the vast army of those who have known Christ for more than ten years and have settled into a stale church life routine. Many of these express a vague feeling of discontentment with their spiritual life, but don't know what to do about it. Others are comfortably asleep and do not even realize that they are barren trees. If you are not bearing fruit right now, you never will unless some of your habits get changed. I will go farther. If you are not bearing evangelistic fruit as a disciple, you are not healthy. Healthy trees produce fruit. Soul winners have a vibrant, growing faith. You can be healthy and fruitful. You can have a huge life of lasting impact. This is God's will for you.

The greatest adventure you and I will ever know in life is to wade into the harvest field and begin working alongside the Father. In the field, the gifts of the Spirit are needed so they flow with mighty force. Most importantly, in the field we get to be with the Father and experience His joy as His lost children come home one by one.

Sherry and I have dedicated the remaining days of our lives to this work. We have no higher desires for our children than that God would use them to win lost people back to God. (They are amazingly effective missionaries already.) Our prayer is that God will use the labor of this writing to help you also move past your fears and hesitations and burst into fruitfulness so we can all hear the Father's booming commendation: "Well done, you good and faithful servant!" Jesus is coming. Let's get to work!

In His Wonderful Love,

*Chuck Quinley*

# 1

# Imagine You Were God

*I*magine that you were the wealthiest and most powerful person on the earth. Fortunately for everyone, you also have the most loving heart. You are determined to use your resources to be a blessing to others. So, every morning you leave the comfort of your majestic home and take your place in a chair, accessible to others who need your assistance. Everyday the line stretches to the horizon, with hundreds upon hundreds lining up to speak to you about their needs.

Their needs are rather repetitious. Most have material needs. They need money or more money, a better job or a home of their own. Some want a car. Some have extravagant requests. They want airplanes, boats and second homes. Everyone feels that they really need everything they ask for and are instantly disappointed if they don't get what they came for.

Some have non-material needs. They need an education or an opportunity. They have some great goal and just want the chance to reach it. A few ask to be noticed by the talent scouts or their bosses when promotion time comes. Others ask for marriage partners or for you to fix a relational difficulty. Many have health problems—cancers, vision problems, deafness. They desperately want to be healed. Day by day, they come and make petitions. You do everything in your power to help them all. You don't want anyone to be overlooked.

## Kidnapped by Your Enemy

But, wealthy as you are, you have a burden of your own. The greatest tragedy imaginable has struck you. Your children are missing. You love them more than life itself.

You have rejoiced over every movement of their lives from birth. Now they are missing and it is all you can think about. If they were only lost you could put out a manhunt, but it's worse than that. Your precious children have been lured away from your bosom and taken captive—kidnapped—not just by a group after money, but by your mortal enemy, a person who hates you with every breath. He cannot hurt you directly because of your immense advantage so he has crafted a plan to hurt you by hurting those you love and would gladly die for.

Your children's fate is predictable. They will be abused constantly. Their promising young lives will become a long ordeal of pain and woe. They will not know kindness. Their every mistake will be held up to them until their little hearts are bruised and filled with conflicting longings and accusations. They will be humiliated alone and in front of others. They will grow to hate their lives. They will cry in the night and will ache in the day, longing for something, but not knowing exactly what because they will not remember their loving Father after a while. They will be raised as the children of the enemy. He will form their self-image and twist them to cause as much damage as possible. All this, to demonstrate his contempt for you. You will never see your children again unless someone helps you find them.

The absolutely astonishing thing is that most of the people in the line know all about this. They know that your children are lost to you and may even have seen them in their neighborhood, school or in the office where they work. Still, they come with shopping list in hand, some returning to the line day after day for more, unmoved and unmindful of the heavy weight of grief you are silently carrying. Your sense of duty compels you and so you take your place regardless, trying to forgive them their callous selfishness in the sight of your private pain. You continue to help them deal with their own lives while yours is in such torment. How would you feel?

I think that's where God is today. We all look to Him as the Big Answer Man. We take to Him our every request, marking each one "Urgent!" We ask for things we need and many other things that we'd be better off without. When He doesn't answer the way we think He should, we get discouraged and sometimes pout. "I've been passed over for promotion three times now. Doesn't God care?!"

Yes, we know about His children. We see their pain-filled lives daily. The devil has them blinded and chained so tightly that they can never free themselves. We resent having to work beside them or having them move next door. We don't need their problems. We step over them like the priest and Levite in the parable of the Good Samaritan, hurrying to get to church to present our latest list to God. We are so caught up in our own little, passing worlds that we do not often stop to contemplate God's world. He's a person, too. He has a heart that feels joy and pain just like we do. Over the lost He has unending pain.

Back to our metaphor. Imagine that one day some young man in the asking line begins to look at your face and tunes into you. He begins to feel the burden that has caused those creases on your forehead and the bags under your eyes. Taking a farewell look at his shopping list, he crumples it up and puts it in his pocket. Then he breaks out of line and comes to the front, causing quite a stir with the others. He walks up, takes you by the hand, looks you in the eyes and says, "I want to help you find your lost children. I have things I want and need too, but they are nothing compared to what is crushing your heart today. What can I do to help you find them and get them safely back home in your arms?"

What would your reaction be? What would you do for such a person? I know what I would do. First, I'd put him to work right away as effectively as possible. Then, after he had truly entered the rescue mission, I would call my most trusted servants and say, "Find out everything about that person. Whatever he needs in life, give it to him so that he won't become distracted and stop the search. As long as he searches for my children provide for him in abundance every day." I think God responds in the same way whenever anyone decides to develop a burden for the lost.

## Pia Was Taken from the Mall

A few months ago, Pia, four years old, was playing at the mall down the street. She and her mother, a single parent, are faithful in our church. Her babysitter became distracted while Pia was playing on a slide. In those few moments of inattention Pia wandered off. Strangers picked her up, put her in their car and took her far away.

I have six kids of my own. Nothing in twenty years of pastoring has ever torn my guts out like this event. Mall security was clueless. As we were frantically scouring the mall in tears and terror, we passed others who were casually eating their ice cream cones, going to the movies, and trying to match fabric for curtains and upholstery. We wanted to scream at them, "Don't you know that Pia is missing! Help us!!!" But we knew that, as much as we loved Pia, it was our personal problem. These people wouldn't help. It didn't concern them.

All we knew to do was cry out to God and ask Him to turn the hearts of the adults who took her and force them to do the right thing and release her. The next afternoon someone called the mall from 45 miles away to say that if anyone wanted the child they could come and get her. God cares about lost children. When we heard the news we couldn't stop the tears.

## Pour Out to Others and I'll Pour in to You

Pastoring in Jamaica, we had a powerful "prayer mother" named Mavis Reid. By the time we moved there she had been fasting and praying every Wednesday for twenty years. Hundreds of people journeyed weekly from across the island to be with her in her fasting service. Miracles were seen in abundance. People were saved and delivered by the hundreds. Churches were planted as a result. Sister Reid became a legend in the churches across the island. She told me how it all started.

> One day I sent my daughter to the corner store to buy on credit a tin of shoe polish and a piece of rope to tie up the pig. She returned empty-handed. The storeowner said that our credit was exhausted. We had to pay cash. I began to fast one day a week to have the spirit of poverty broken from my family and I began to see some breakthroughs. The amazing things, however, began to happen after the Lord spoke to me one Wednesday and said, 'If you will stop focusing on your family alone, and start praying with that much energy for the needs of others. I will surely take care of your family.' From that day on, I declared Wednesday as a day of prayer and fasting for the needs of others.

When Mavis Reid and her disciples gathered weekly to fast and pray for the needs of others, amazing things always happened. I was there the day our simple Mavis Reid laid her powerful prayer hands on the ambassador of the United States and prayed for his heart to be guided into right paths. He received it with joy. I saw policemen stop their patrol cars and come inside the church hall on Wednesdays so the group could pray for their protection, provision and integrity. We heard weekly testimonies about families restored, bodies healed, and life opportunities granted. It all happened because one person decided to get out of the begging line and come alongside the heart of God to be taught how to care for others.

## A Heart Like His

The great miracles of Jesus all start with the same words: "He had compassion on them and. . ." Compassion for the lost doesn't come naturally to any of us because we are selfish from birth. We have to want to become compassionate. We have to ask God to place the burdens of His great heart within us. We have to actively yield to the movings and directions of the Holy Spirit as He arranges coincidences and circumstances so that we encounter those who are earnestly seeking for Him.

Our Bible says, "The heart of the king is in the hand of the Lord and He turns it any direction He wants." (Prov. 21:1) Ask the Father to turn your heart right now. If God can turn the hearts of the people who took Pia from the mall, how much more easily can He turn our hearts when we want Him to? Stop right now and pray. Ask Him to break your heart with the things that break His. Ask Him to make you love what He loves and hate what He hates.

## An Exercise

Why not try an exercise? Go to a mall and, as you walk, look at people. I mean *really* see them. As you look at them make a conscious effort to say in your mind, "Oh you dear one, unless someone finds you in time, you will never see your Father." Do this regularly as you drive or go to school or work. The heart of God will gradually form within you. There's no need to start "witnessing" until our heart is spilling over with God's love and compassion for the lost. "We know that we live in him and he in us, because he has given us of his Spirit. We love because He first loved us" (1 John 4:13, 19 NIV). Ask God for His Spirit and His love for the lost today.

# 2

# Building Churches
# or Winning the Lost?

*A*young lady, full of potential and anointing, looked across the table at me and said, *"I'm so sick of my Christian life. Church, church, church. All we do is go to church, sit and pay tithes. I have things inside me that have to come out! I want to make a difference! I tell this to my pastor and he offers to let me teach a children's class at Sunday school. There has to be more!"* Many mature believers experience the same frustration whether they express it this forcefully or not.

Many of today's churches are like saltshakers. Culinary experts will tell you that the purpose of salt is to influence the taste of the other ingredients in our food. We pour it into saltshakers where it remains clean and white, waiting with all the other salt granules for its chance to "make a difference" in the meal. So far, so good. But what if the cook became fixated on accumulating salt instead of producing flavorful meals that satisfied the hungry? He would buy progressively larger and more glorious salt shakers into which he could pour more and more salt that would sit, well-preserved but effectively wasted because it never accomplished its purpose.

Jesus said that we were supposed to be the salt of the *world*, not the salt of the church. Modern churches have done a great job gathering the Christian salt into some amazing saltshakers. We have, without a doubt, the most expansive salt-handling devices ever seen in the history of God's people. We have created music, publishing, counseling and even vacation industries geared exclusively for Christians to keep them happy as they all sit together, unpolluted from the world. We sit together in the same section at the ballpark, take "Christian" cruises, go to amusement parks on special "church outing" days and attend "Christian concerts" focusing so much on our own Christian well being, some have completely forgotten our calling to be salt in the world.

## What Jesus Taught about the Church

A few months ago I was asked to teach a course on ecclesiology, the doctrine of the church. What I learned while preparing for the course was a real eye-opener. Jesus did not teach anything about the church. I don't mean that he treated it as a *minor* theme. I mean, he never gave a teaching about it—not, the importance of big churches or small churches, how to plant churches or how to market the church. Not a word about ushers, choirs, corporate documents, buildings, boards, cantatas or sermons. Nothing. Only Matthew even records the word, "church" coming out of Christ's mouth and then only twice. In Matthew 16:18, Christ makes a prediction that *he* will build it. In chapter eighteen, Jesus makes a passing reference to how we are to maintain harmony and discipline as we live together as a community, Outside of these two passages, Jesus never spoke about the church as a thing in itself. I can't believe that I never noticed it in 20 years of reading the Bible. I was so busy trying to build churches that I just assumed that my focus was right.

Humans tend to make idols out of anything their hands can build and pastors, in general, are no different from most folks. I think that over the last 30 years, we pastors have been seduced by the "success culture" of our generation and have, consequently, produced the most excellent church machinery ever. We have multimillion-dollar facilities, highly sophisticated master planning and some of the finest sound and visual equipment ever made. Want to know a secret? Most of us pastors hate the monster we have created. (Remember please, that I pastor well over 1,000 people). In truth, we hate being expected to know about so many different fields of work (psychology, construction, publishing, social work, ancient manuscripts, etc.). We hate the meetings, the paperwork, the business-like atmosphere of the office and facing some of the pampered, perpetual "me-first" babies we now have to pacify. But more than anything in the world, we hate being so busy from running the machine that we can't pray and hear God speak. Many of us feel trapped, and so we run from conference to conference trying to find a way out.

Here's the way out. Jesus never taught about the church because the church is a given. It will exist anywhere God is active. The people God calls will answer His voice and automatically gather themselves together in worship around leaders who can help them develop and teach them God's word. Believers will always love fellowship, good teaching and doing ministry together. Jesus did not present the church as some thing for us to build. It builds itself (Eph. 4:16). When we take control and try to build it ourselves, we profane it and invite disease.

## Where Jesus Focused His Ministry

Jesus was focused on people. Individuals. Cities. He walked each day with "harvest eyes," connecting with people everywhere he went. When he opened his eyes he saw the lost—seas of lost people—lost people everywhere! He saw that they were sincerely seeking to make themselves right, happy and whole, but that they were clueless as to how to really do it.

Lost people are sheep without a shepherd. They follow the other sheep and hope for the best. Satan destroys them by the thousands each day. The busy churchmen of Christ's day were blind to them, but Jesus saw them. Nothing else was more important.

So, don't think about the choir, the youth retreat or the golden-agers classroom with rocking chairs. Just focus on lost people. Everybody in the church, focus on the lost. Pastors, elders and teachers, focus on the lost. Children's leaders, focus on the lost. Youth workers, focus on the lost. Ushers and parking-lot attendants, focus on the lost. Man in the pew, grandmothers, and baby Christian, focus on the lost. Evangelize the lost and disciple them to maturity. We have no other purpose as a church.

If we need buildings, equipment, magazines and radio stations (and we do) God will provide them. We will want to gather and worship, pray and soak up the rich word of God, but remember, we were never called to build the church. We were called to take up the only unfinished ministry of Jesus—seeking and saving the lost. Do this and you will be happy, blessed and living under the smile of the Father.

Let's bring God's lost children back home to Him. He cares about little else in these last days. It will take effort and sacrifice, the biggest of which is to daily step out of the comfortable, "don't-bother-me-I-have-enough-to-do-already" life we have all created. We can change if we want to.

## God Only Has One Problem

Most believers who have been saved for over ten years are utterly barren evangelistically. Worse yet, they will never bear fruit again. Why? They have settled comfortably into their church world, surrounded by God's wonderful children, spoiled by their shepherds and incapable of opening the Bible and explaining salvation accurately to a lost person. They have come to see the body of Christ as a divided house: those who are called and those who are not. Pastors and evangelists, for example, are called to do the "reaching people" sort of things. The rest of us are not. So, believers by the millions attend church regularly, then invest the remainder of their earthly lives engaged in other loves: work, sports, food, family, hobbies. Many of them may feel guilty about it (I know because I did for many years until I entered the harvest myself.) but precious few will ever leave their comfort zones.

In evangelism, God has only one problem—and it's not the harvest. God's only trouble in reaching the lost is the ratio of harvest workers to receptive people. Jesus said to his inwardly focused, sometimes-exclusivist disciples, "Wake up! Open your eyes and look at this harvest! It is already ripe and ready to be reached!"

## The Need is the Call

Bill Wilson is a man who has devoted his life to taking the gospel to children while they are young and soft. He realizes that lost children don't come to Sunday school, so he goes to them. With hundreds of volunteers, he holds sidewalk Sunday Schools throughout New York City. Someone once asked him about his calling. How did he know God was calling him to evangelize children of the street? His reply stunned them. "I wasn't called. I saw the need and knew I had to help. The need is the call."

Think about that for a minute. "The need is the call." In the parable of the Good Samaritan there are three men. Two are steeped in a religious subculture of church attendance. They step over the wounded, bleeding man. They aren't called to this. It isn't their ministry. The last man in the story is a businessman on an important trip. He also isn't called to be a professional paramedic. He's just a guy on his way to a sales conference. But he sees the need and realizes that the need is a call from God that he must answer. He puts his schedule on hold, attends to the wounded man in a personal and practical way and then continues on his journey—but he is forever bonded to that man he rescued. He enters into the empathy of God and feels just a bit of God's fatherly concern and the joy of loving in deeds, not words. No Bible study. No church service. He's just in the world, being salt, and Jesus approves of his life and the way he used the sovereign power of choice God has given to each of us.

You can be a person like that, and in your deepest heart you know that you want to. You know that it is right and that if you can get past your fears and selfishness this could be a wonderful adventure. You could make some memories for eternity!

## Harvesting the Earth with God

When I was eighteen I committed my life to Christ after a wild and rebellious teen life. Shortly thereafter, I felt led to spend my life as a pastor. The next summer, I went to a Braves baseball game and saw Atlanta-Fulton County stadium packed with fans. In a quiet moment between innings I began to try and focus on the crowd that I had largely tuned out before. I tried to see their faces and wondered what their lives were like. The Lord spoke to me at that moment and said, "In your life you will win that many people to me." I was shocked and astonished. Me, reach thousands of lost people? Although I sincerely loved the Lord, I had never led even one person to him. I wanted to, but my efforts were always so tense and pressured that my stomach ached and the other person never seemed to respond.

Sixteen years ago, my wife, Sherry, and I waded into the harvest field under God's leadership and have never known more joy. Every time our church world starts to drain our energy and peace, we just refocus on these simple lessons about harvesting the earth, and our lives get back into focus as the Spirit fills us and allows us to bear fruit for the Father. We want you to know this joy and to enter into the life you were called to enjoy.

## You Can Bear Fruit!

In Ephesians 2:10, Paul wrote: "For we are God's workmanship, created in Christ Jesus to do good works, which God prepared in advance for us to do." Jesus told his disciples, "You did not choose me, but I chose you and appointed you to go and bear fruit—fruit that will last." (John 15:16) Fruit bearing is the sign of a true disciple (John 15:8) and is the only purpose for God to extend our lives upon the earth. You can bear fruit, abundant fruit! This is true no matter what kind of personality you have, no matter where you work or whether you are a pastor or a layperson. You can bear fruit in your daily life without knocking on doors or handing out tracts randomly or arguing religion with hard-hearted people.

There are millions of sincere, searching people out there. Their sighs come up to God as prayers begging Him to send someone to tell them how to find peace. God will answer their prayers with you. He will arrange coincidences to seat you together or to connect on the chat line. He will give you the words and the power to speak for Him, but we have to present ourselves to Him as workers who show up for work.

Proverbs 10:5 declares, "He who sleeps during harvest time is a disgraceful son." Well, friends, it's harvest time. After this harvest has come in, there will never be another one. God needs you. His need is our call. As Christ's disciples, we don't *have* to ever sing a solo, teach Sunday school or preach to a large crowd. We don't ever *have* to lead a Bible study, lead a ministry team or sit on a board or committee. But you and I <u>do</u> have to respond to God's need for harvest workers or we will be disgraceful children.

## Harvesting Is a Joy, not a Burden

I grew up in the city, but my dad was raised in the farmland of lower Alabama (jokingly referred to as L.A.). Every summer we entered into the required ritual of planting a garden in our back yard. Honestly, I didn't find it interesting or enjoyable. I knew it was needed and that farming was a noble thing to do. It was also hot, hard work and I couldn't wait until the day was done. When I became an adult, however, I found that I was drawn to the soil too. I planted my own garden at our first house and I discovered that no tomato could ever taste better than the four-inch-wide "Big Boy" you pluck from the vine yourself and eat with saltshaker in hand, standing barefoot in your garden.

You see, clearing land, turning the soil, and sowing seed are not fun, but the harvest itself is a thing of supreme joy. Painful preparation work is faithfully done in anticipation of the generous payoff of the harvest. Planting indeed draws blood, tears and sweat, but harvesting is done with singing and laughter! God is calling you and me into harvest work. Christ and others have already done the groundbreaking and seed sowing for thousands of years before us. We have the great blessing of living in the generation of the last great harvest of the earth. Consequently, we have the great opportunity of simply entering into the painful labors of others and reaping the payoff! This soul harvest was prophesied in Revelation 14:15–16:

> *Then another angel came out of the temple and called*
> *in a loud voice to him who was sitting on the cloud,*

*"Take your sickle and reap, because the time to reap has come, for the harvest of the earth is ripe." So he who was seated on the cloud swung his sickle over the earth, and the earth was harvested.* (NIV)

You might not know it, but more people came to Christ in the decades of the 1980's and 90's than in the 2000 year history of the church combined. It is harvest time saints! So, come on, get up off the Church-life couch and let's enter the harvest together. Why not stop now and have a time of prayer before you read farther, telling God all about your hang-ups and asking Him to make a joy-filled harvest worker out of you? Your life will never be boring or unfulfilling again, because you will become a fellow-worker with God Himself in His field. He works there every day.

# 3

# Conquest Evangelism:
## The PFC's Come
## to Town

*T*he blue, airport-style Dodge van pulled into the church parking lot. Our pastor had announced the week before that the "Pioneers for Christ" from Lee College were coming to our church to lead us on an evangelistic invasion of our town. Military metaphors abounded. It was spiritual war. We were going to invade the devil's territory and rescue Satan's prisoners. Recruits were called for and I raised my hand.

Reporting for duty that Saturday, I was led into the fellowship hall for the briefing on the day's combat strategy. We green recruits were to accompany the seasoned war veterans from the PFC's who did this practically every weekend. We were taught the standard operating procedures for approaching houses, entering and making conversation with the resident to lead them to the Lord. If they were heavies, like Jehovah's Witnesses, we were to drop back and let the PFC's debate them skillfully. As we left the church, we were supplied with gospel tracts as ammunition and were reminded to carry our Bibles (the big gun).

Like paratroopers, we jumped out of the van on our appointed corners and were assured that we wouldn't be abandoned on the field of battle. The van would return at 1 P.M. and bring us some lunch. Clutching my bible timidly, and thankful that I didn't know anyone who lived in the trailer park, I followed in the wake of the extroverted young lady who was my leader. We knocked on doors all morning. My introversion was agonizing as we invaded the homes of others again and again. I have to say that my leader was great at this. She didn't hesitate to begin conversations and was genuinely interested in the lives of those we encountered. Many were suspicious. Some were rude. Others appreciated the attention so much that they wanted us to stay; but we never visited for long. We came to "evangelize," not to make friendships. We had other trailers to visit and when the day was done, we would all count homes contacted and how many people had received a tract or prayed to receive the Lord.

By the end of the day, amazingly, we had had many meaningful conversations. Quite a few people had agreed to pray the "sinner's prayer" that insured salvation. We rejoiced privately every time someone would pray this prayer along with us. "Wow! That's three that have been saved already!" We sincerely wanted the lost to be found. (That's the only reason we had devoted our precious Saturday to this mission). By 4 P.M., the day was done. We gathered at the church for a debriefing, swapped war stories and tallied the number of homes reached. The next day they announced the dozens who had received Christ during the invasion, and everyone shouted, "Hallelujah!"

Nobody seemed to notice that these converts weren't in church with us. I don't think anyone ever went to see who or how they were. I think we all felt better about ourselves for having sacrificed for the Lord. We just privately hoped that the "sinner's prayer" had worked for them.

## Conquest Evangelism

Most of our models of evangelism are based on conquest. Like Sonny, in Robert Duvall's film, <u>The Apostle,</u> we often treat evangelism as impersonally as war. In war, for example, you "demonize" your enemy. That is, you don't think of him as a person. You don't consider that he has a mother, wife or kids or that he is scared. You have to conquer him because he's bad and you are good.

I once heard Loren Cunningham, founder of Youth With A Mission, tell the story of a time when he was staying in a house with another leader in missions. Two Jehovah's Witnesses knocked on their door and asked to come in. These JW's had no idea that they were dealing with men so well-versed in the Bible and in the cult's own teachings that they had written guides on how to deal with this cult. It was clear that the witnesses had come to make war on their Christian faith, and the debate was soon intense. These witnesses had never dealt with anyone like these two men, and soon they were confused and contradicting themselves repeatedly. Finally, in exasperation and humiliation, they left the house, heads hung low in defeat.

Loren Cunningham is a man of God known for his humility and honesty. He recounted that as their defeated adversaries limped down the road, and he and the other minister were high-fiving each other the Lord spoke to him, saying simply, "You lost." Loren replied, "But Lord, what do you mean? We seem to have won convincingly." The Lord replied, "You lost because you were affected by the spirit of these men. They came here to argue religion. Within minutes they had influenced you and you were no more a man of peace. You lost to the spirit that motivated them because you took on their ways as your own."

We all need to take this lesson to heart. Paul reminded us that the weapons we fight with are not the weapons of the world and that we must not make war the way the world does. Too many people think of evangelism as winning an argument, wearing the other person down, making them to confess their sins, defeating them. "They lose. We win. Glory to God!" This is human pride and self-righteousness and it has nothing to do with evangelism and everything to do with our need to feel important and significant.

The most awful abuses in the history of the world have been committed by the religious—whether it is the Hindu fanatic, the Muslim terrorist or the Christian crusader. Power and religion are a poisonous mixture. The self-righteous are almost beyond the reach of God because they profane the very instruments of God's grace on a daily basis. Jesus was crucified by religious clerics, not prostitutes and thieves. That's why Jesus taught us that the door to salvation, like the proverbial "needle's eye" in the city walls of Jerusalem, can only be reached by crawling on our knees with our head bowed low. The first beatitude is "Blessed are those who are poor in spirit . . ." (i.e., those who recognize that they are utterly dependent upon the mercy of God for their salvation) "for theirs is the kingdom of heaven." (Matt. 5:3 NIV)

Self-righteous, legalistic people make pathetic evangelists. They hurt tender people with their harsh words and judgmental pronouncements. They do not know the heart of God, nor do they have that heart within them. They just want to be right and prove that others are wrong. That makes them feel good.

## The Law of Love

Every pedigreed animal has defining marks. A collie can never be confused with a beagle, even on a dark night. Jesus said that his true disciples would all have one defining mark. Their color and language would all be different. Their choice of food or clothing style would probably never match. They might not necessarily have much in common, humanly speaking, but they would all have the divine birthmark: agape love.

Jesus said: "By this all men will know that you are my disciples, if you love (agape in the Greek) one another." (John 13:35 NIV) Someone advised me early as a believer that I should read 1 John every day until I memorized and lived it. My favorite part is, "He who does not love (agape) does not know God for God is love (agape.)" (1 John 4:8) John goes on to say that while it is possible to fake a churchy form of righteousness, you can't fake agape love for long. It is too costly and irritating to the fleshly person. On the other hand, there is no man with such an iron constitution that he can hold inside the love of God if it is present inside of him.

I won't go into a long discussion about the nature of agape, but you and I need to recognize that agape doesn't carry with it the understanding of warm, fuzzy feelings. Agape simply means that we put the welfare of others first. We do the thing that will minister to them whether we feel like it or not. It is a conscious decision, a willful choice to let our best side rule even if our inner selfish brat screams all the way through it. The Good Samaritan saw a man in blood. He cleaned his wounds and took him to a shelter. That's agape, whether he felt anything that day or not.

Evangelism is agape. It is something you do out of kindness to those who are lost and may not even know it. Agape always calls for the investment of yourself. It will always cost you something; but because it is the center of the character of God, living in agape will change you into the kind of person even you will be amazed to know.

Conquest evangelism doesn't care to know a person's name. Jesus cares about everyone. He even asked demons their name. His greatest recorded miracles are generally prefaced with the words, "Jesus had compassion on them and so he. . . ." Let me tell you from personal experience that if you will simply open your heart INTENTION-ALLY to love lost people and INTENTIONALLY establish loving, positive, personal relationships with them, God will gradually build a burden of compassion in your heart that will make evangelism the most emotionally rewarding experience of your life. You will not dread it, because love will compel you. You will not want to win. You will want *them* to win over the darkness that holds them captive.

The problem with the PFC approach wasn't so much that we entered strange neighborhoods and knocked on doors introducing ourselves as messengers of God. It was that we left those homes that opened their doors to us and never went back. We violated the law of love. Nothing that violates that law, even in the name of the Lord, can ever fulfill the will of God.

In the next chapter, I will share how God, in His mercy, delivered my wife and myself from the world of the religious and opened the doors to a harvest of the lost that has allowed us to see 13 of our neighbors become an exciting, happy congregation of 1,300 despite persecution, setbacks and human mistakes.

# 4

# The World of the Lost

*I* knew a guy in college named Randy. Randy was blind. Somehow in his youth, his eyes had been destroyed in an explosion. One day, I watched Randy going down the familiar sidewalk, tap-tap-tapping along with his red-tipped cane. He was far across the campus from me, but I could still see him zipping along the sidewalk. Too late, I realized what was about to happen. Someone had parked a large panel truck across the sidewalk to unload some supplies at the campus bookstore. All I could do from my distant perch was to watch in pity as Randy crashed, face-first, into the sidewall of the trailer bed. He was stunned by the unexpected blow and staggered back a few steps. His cane began sweeping wildly in front of him, hitting nothing (he was between the wheeled sections so it was clear below). He tried again. Crash! He turned left and tried to walk. Farther left. Then right. Farther right. Right again. I could see his frustration. In front of him from the waist up was an impassible wall of sheet metal. There was simply no way to get through to the other side except to enter the busy street on the left, or to walk sideways across the steep stairs leading down to the campus store. (Finally, someone closer saw what was happening and called to him. He could do nothing but wait for someone to help him.)

## Lost in the Woods

Have you ever been in a situation where there was nothing you could do but cry for help and wait in hopes that some good Samaritan would rescue you? A few years ago the papers carried a story of some folks from the city who decided to go cross-country skiing in Colorado. Two of them had been on a great trip the year before and the others now wanted to experience the same. They drove as far as their cars could go and then strapped packs on their backs with all their essentials. They skied through the deep evergreen forest for hours, hoping to arrive at a cabin deep in the woods just before dark. A fork in the trail forced them to make a decision. One from last year said they should turn left. The other, with a stronger personality, declared that he was the leader and that he remembered perfectly well that it was right; so they followed him, the expert. Hours later and hopelessly lost, they realized that they would have to spend the night in the snow. One of the members had been struggling with her gear earlier and had been convinced to abandon her pack to keep up. She suffered a horrible night in the cold.

Four nights later they were rescued by volunteers who had searched for days until they found them and brought them home. It cost the state of Colorado over $200,000, but they were found at last, cold, but still alive. These lost skiers had no way of rescuing themselves. They had to hope that others cared enough to look for them until they were found.

## Lost at Sea

Similarly, a fireman from Philadelphia and his wife went along with another couple for a dream vacation in Cancun, Mexico. While there, the men decided to rent jet skis and have an adventure at sea. They saved money by avoiding the better-named shops and choosing to rent the more banged-up equipment of a small outfit farther down the beach, away from the trafficked areas. The storeowners held their credit cards as a guarantee for the jet skis and waved cheerfully as the men sprinted across the bay. Most people stay near the shore, but, being brave American men, these two headed out to the horizon, miles from shore, zigzagging and enjoying the exhilaration of this hot sport. That's when the true adventure began. The jet ski of the fireman stopped working. His brother-in-law came along side to help. They tried repeatedly to crank the engine, but it was dead. "Those jerks! Probably out of gas!" Having nothing to tow him with, the brother-in-law decided to return to the shop and get a rope or a mechanic or a replacement jet ski. Reluctantly, the other accepted the plan.

The brother-in-law had trouble getting any sympathy from the shop owners who simply reminded him that he was liable for all damages. By the time they returned to look for his partner, he had traveled miles in the Gulf currents and was nowhere to be found. It was hard to say exactly where he had been anyway. The horizon is a pretty big place. The lost man's frantic wife stayed on the phone with the U.S. embassy, trying to get someone to organize the Coast Guard to find her missing husband who, they hoped, was still floating on the jet ski (which had been leaking). Six days later they were still trying to find the stranded man.

Thankfully, the story has a happy ending. The jet-skier was rescued at sea a week later, covered in boils and serious sunburn, and dehydrated. He had had some horrifying encounters with sharks that had circled him at times while he floated helplessly in the Gulf of Mexico. This man was saved because the people who loved him refused to stop searching for him until he was found, and because a captain cared enough to go through the ordeal of stopping his large merchant vessel to help someone in distress.

## Lost People Can't Help Themselves

These two stories illustrate the real predicament of a truly lost person: they are completely helpless to save themselves. If they knew what to do they would do it, but they are lost and out of options. All they can do is try to hang on to whatever is available near them until help arrives. Then they will scream and wave with all their might.

The smartest guy I've ever met is a medical doctor/artist/author/swimmer, etc., named Laurence Anderson from New Zealand. He told me a story about blindness that amazes me still. It's a medical case study about an older lady who checked into a hospital complaining that she was constantly falling down around her house. She thought it had something to do with her balance. After thoroughly examining her, the doctor met with her and her daughter in her hospital room. "We have examined you and find that there is nothing at all wrong with your balance or inner ear. Your problem, I'm afraid, is that you are completely blind." The woman became irritated. "Ridiculous! I can see everything perfectly! Look, over there to my right is a window. In front of me is a door. The TV is mounted to the wall up to my left." She was right in every detail. The doctor asked one other question, "Describe me and what I am wearing." "Well, you have on a doctor's coat, pens in your pocket and a stethoscope around your neck." The daughter said softly, "Sorry, Mom, he is wearing casual clothes, no coat—none of that stuff. It's true. I promise." The patient sat in stunned silence. "How do I see, then, if I am blind?" The doctor explained to her that we don't see with our eyes; they only take in signals. We "see" with our brain as it inverts the image on the retina, and interprets the signals into something we are familiar with. She could see the window because she felt the sunlight on her skin. She heard the door in front and the familiar hospital-style mounted TV coming from above and her brain generated a mental picture of all those stimuli. She was, in fact, truly blind in her eyes, though she thought she could see perfectly.

## Blinded by Satan

That's the challenge of spiritual lostness. We are certain that we can see, even though the devil has blinded our minds completely.

> *"The god of this age (Satan) has blinded the minds of unbelievers, so that they cannot see the light of the gospel of the glory of Christ who is the image of God."* (2 Co. 4:4 NIV)

Let's look at this text carefully. First of all, we see that un-believers are blind, like Randy, except that their blindness isn't physical, but mental. Their eyes see perfectly well, but their minds are blinded. They think they can see, but really they cannot. The passage also tells us that:

- Their blindness is not an accident
- They were blinded by Lucifer, God's enemy, so they will be lost forever
- They cannot (note, can not) see the glory of Christ without outside help.
- Somebody has to rescue them.

The entire book of Romans is a missions letter from the Apostle Paul to a collection of house churches informing them of his plan to evangelize the people of Spain. He asks them for prayers and financial support. In order to help them understand why the church needs to be con-sumed with reaching the lost, he spends chapter after chapter exploring the total lostness of man and the wonder-ful offer of a salvation by grace, based on the shed blood of Jesus alone. His argument for missions comes to its cli-max in chapter ten, which basically makes one big point: Lost People Cannot Help Themselves.

> *"Everyone who calls on the name of the Lord will be saved. [But] How then can they call on the one they*

> *have not believed in? And how can they believe in*
> *the one of whom they have not heard? And how can*
> *they hear with out someone preaching to them?*
> (Romans 1:13–14, NIV, parenthesis mine)

Do you see it? Without anyone's assistance, a lost person can find witchcraft, New Age philosophy, materialism, agnosticism and any cult group you care to mention, but they cannot find Christ without outside help. Why? Remember, they are spiritually blind. Their minds "make sense" of this life in a manner consistent with their being bound in sin and under the spiritual control of the evil enemy of God. They just can't see the truth, and don't have an appetite for it. It is not within them to comprehend it without outside help.

## It's Hard to See Jesus because of the Church

Try to imagine that you are with a person who doesn't know one verse from the Bible. She doesn't know the story of Abraham, Noah, or even David and Goliath. (If you are having a hard time imagining anyone being in this category it is probably because you've been insulated from the real world by your Christian sub-culture. Believe it or not, half the world has never heard the name of Jesus. We even met a girl from California once who honestly didn't know the story of Adam and Eve.) Now, in that frame of mind, turn on Christian TV and try to imagine, from their perspective, what it must look like: Men with strangely swept hairdos, giving animated speeches to crowds who seem to idolize them and laugh uncontrollably at their every joke as if following cues; hyped program intros and promises too good to be true and money, money, money! Then they come to church and try to follow songs like, "As the deer panteth for the water so my heart longeth after thee" (What?!) Or how about this one, "They rush on the city, they run on the walls, great is the army that carries out his word!" (This happy-sounding scripture song is about the Jewish army scaling the walls of a closed city to burn it and put to death everyone inside, so I'm actually glad they don't understand it.)

I'm not trying to mock these idiosyncratic Christian habits, but I am simply illustrating why lost people often cannot comprehend the jewel of Jesus, even when they try to approach Christianity. Often, our presentation of Jesus is wrapped up in a church culture that takes decades to absorb and appreciate, so that lost people can't really see him for who he is because of all our added stuff. We think nothing of it because it is our culture; but they are spiritually blind, and many things we find wonderful are actually walls to them (like the well-intentioned truck that prevented Randy from making progress on his journey).

## *How Do We Rescue Them?*
### *Focus on the Receptive*

Luke, chapter ten, is the definitive teaching from Jesus about how to evangelize. In verse ten, he tells us what to do when confronted by someone who doesn't want to hear about Jesus, salvation or their sin. Ready for the Master's instruction? Leave them alone. That's all. Just leave them alone. Don't argue, nag, or slip them tracts secretly. Don't bother them or harass them in any way. Jesus has given us permission to completely avoid repeated confrontations with hardened people. There's wisdom in this. (This also eliminates the most common fear that keeps us from being a light to others—the fear of rejection.)

I have seen hundreds of people leave the spiritual darkness and turn lovingly toward Christ. Ninety-nine percent of them were facing a personal search or crisis of some sort at the time they opened up to accept Jesus as Lord. The reality is this: every lost person goes through cycles of receptivity and resistance. The man who is full of pride today can easily become humbled by life's circumstances by next month. Don't write him off, but don't fill his mind with negative stereotypes of Christians as irritating, argumentative, self-righteous bigots by trying to coerce him into salvation before he's ready. Later in the book I'll offer you a simple four step daily pattern of life that will position you to spend your time and energy sharing about Jesus informally with receptive people only.

### Four Levels of Lostness

I think its fair to say that there are four main types of lost people, whether in spiritual or natural terms. (For the sake of discussion, let's call them "levels of lostness.")

*Level #1: "I'm lost but I don't know it."* People who are lost at this level are totally unaware of it. Like the skiers who got lost in the woods, for example. The minute they took one step toward the trail on the right they were lost, whether they knew it or not. Lost people are all on the wrong road. That is the truth, whether they are aware of it or not. The problem is that only those who are truly humble and teachable can be corrected at this point. Because there are no consequences to being lost yet, they feel no alarm and are naturally resistant to suggestions that they might have made a mistake in their lives. They see no indications, as yet, that they are on the wrong road. There are no disasters and they feel no pain.

*Level #2: " I'm starting to feel a bit disoriented."* People at this level are looking for familiar landmarks and don't see them. They aren't sure that they are off the proper pathway, but they are starting to question. If we had encountered the firefighter on his jet ski five minutes after his partner had left him and had asked if he was in need of help, he probably would have waved us off. "It's ok. I have the situation under control." One hour later, he would still have been able to see the hotels, but would definitely have been doing some thinking about finding a way to get closer to the shoreline that was slowly disappearing.

Spiritually, people begin to search when they leave what is familiar. They feel disoriented when they move away from home, get married, have children, change jobs, and deal with a death or in any way face a radical change in their engrained patterns of living. Undergoing education is always a time of leaving familiar thoughts and paradigms behind and forming new ones. People in any kind of transition are generally more open to dialogue, even though they may not be ready to admit that they are lost and in need of a Savior. Just sow positive, loving seeds into their lives at this stage. These seeds will ultimately ripen into a harvest of accurate spiritual direction in their lives when the time is right.

*Level #3: "I am beginning to fear what will happen to me if my present state continues. I admit that I am lost and need help.* People at this level eagerly accept help from anyone. Their pride is no longer a barrier. They are in trouble and they know it. Without help they cannot find their way, so they begin to actively search for the right path. Cult groups target people at this point because they are vulnerable and open to anyone, even if the doctrine they represent is strange and unbelievable, or their demands are overbearing. As God's "Search and Rescue Team" we have to keep our eyes open daily for these precious ones. They are actively seeking help from many sources. Their spiritual search is intense, fueled by their inner pain and fear. They read books, listen to tapes and attend self-improvement seminars in hope of finding help. Whether they can accurately define their hunger or not, they are searching for God. Reaching people at this level requires only the willingness to do so. They are ready.

*Level #4: "I am screaming for help in a blind panic."* These people are the ones in the "dramatic testimonies" section of your Christian magazines. They are eagerly crying out to leave their life of drugs, severe depression, prostitution, or physical abuse. They are totally out of control as persons and are instantly grateful and passionate about the Lord and the ones he used to rescue them. Among our church's inner circle of caregivers we call such people EGRs. It stands for "Extra Grace Required," because people in this state are often so desperate for help that they cling too tightly and ignore the normal boundaries of personal space that ministers need in order to function in the ministry as a lifetime vocation. We remind everyone we train that they will have to be extra-sensitive with people like this, because their lives have turned into a nightmare and it is understandable that they will demand almost exclusive attention for a while. In time, the security of the Christian family calms their fears, and the power of Jesus leads them to a new birth and to the power of a recreated, Spirit-filled life. They will normalize at that point. For now, just hold them tightly and comfort them. You are their hero and they will never forget what you have done for them.

From the hard-hearted to the panic stricken, you and I encounter lost people every day of our lives. As we go out to do whatever our schedule calls for, let us also determine to stay tuned to God's "emergency radio frequency" at all times. We will inevitably be led to someone who is calling out for Him. That's the beginning of our mission.

# 5

# Jamaica, Jamaica

*J*amaica! Just the name conjures up images of a tropical paradise: balmy ocean breezes caressing your skin as you lay on pristine white beaches and watch swaying coconut trees moving to the pulsating rhythms of Reggae music. The travel posters advertising holidays in this sunny paradise do not begin to capture the beauty of the island. Jamaican resorts are fun places with a laid back, good-natured staff that keep you laughing throughout your short holiday. Jamaica is a fun country, a place to let your hair down.

Jamaica is also a deeply traditional and conservative society—something that is lost on casual tourists. Social etiquette is still determined by Victorian-era customs. There is a strong vertical nature to most social relationships. If you are an educated person or someone with a white-collar job, strangers on the street will call you "Boss." Jamaica was a wonderful and challenging place to begin our missions ministry.

The call to Jamaica came on a snowy afternoon in Pennsylvania. At the ripe old age of 23, I received a phone call at the church where we served as youth pastors. The voice on the other end asked if I would be interested in moving to Jamaica to pastor.

I suppose we had to be crazy to consider it. Jamaica has a history of election violence. Castro communism in the 70's had a powerful influence on the youth of Jamaica, increasing racial tensions as a strategy for destabilizing the nation. Many youths were openly hateful of white people as a whole because of the legacy of slavery. (I can't keep a tan over 3 days, no matter how hard I try, so I knew I was doomed.) Nevertheless, after praying we felt that it was definitely the will of God for us to go there.

Our reception from our new congregation (our first solo pastorate) was mixed. Some felt that we were much too young (you aren't respected in Jamaica till you have gray hair), but most were so demonstrative in their love for us that we soon felt we had a family there. We had one child then, Andrew, born just six months before this adventure began. He was soon parroting "Yah Mon!" and chattering on in the patois he picked up from the kids around him. Grammy Birthright adopted him and held him each Sunday so Sherry could teach the children. Bro. and Sis. Reid parented us. Sis. Ida Francis came to see me every Sunday before church to give me a motherly kiss, pinch my cheeks and tell me how handsome I was and that I was going to preach a great message that day because they would all be praying for me.

Our church people were colorful in dress and personality. They clapped long and hard with half a dozen rhythms at one time. Sherry loved sitting with the teenage girls, trying to follow in their hand-clapping patterns. When it really got going, it sounded like a steam locomotive rolling through the large church house. We pastored a Pentecostal church, the Mandeville New Testament Church of God. I loved the personal interactions with the people and the eager, conversational audience for Sunday preaching (there's no such thing as a rhetorical question in a sermon given to a Jamaican church), but I soon learned that there were many rules governing my behavior because of the position I held at the church.

This first became apparent when we were working on a building one day and needed more cement. I walked to the car in my work clothes to proceed to the hardware store when an elder stopped me. "Oh pastor," he said with great concern and respect, "You cannot go to the store like that!" "Why not?" I replied. "Oh, you represent the entire church and must never be seen in public unless you are dressed well." I had to go home, take a shower and change into nice clothes. Only then could I go to the dusty hardware store to order cement. Then I came back to the job, changed clothes again, and resumed work.

Pastors, you see, are like magistrates in Jamaican society. It is one of the most respected roles in a society in which every man deeply craves respect and honor. We did our best to live up to the expectations. Sherry never wore jewelry or makeup, pants, or shorts. I had to remember that I was now a public figure and that the eyes of the town were upon me and that they judged the church by my actions. I soon learned that the ones who judged the most, however, were the members of other churches whose opinions and words were so quickly taken to heart by the members of our own growing flock.

### Jamaica, Jamaica Resort

By our fourth year, we had discovered that missionary life is hard, grueling work. The cultural adjustments were severe at times. It is sort of like being forced to write well with your left hand when you are right-handed. After a while, it just irritates you to have to be "contrary" to yourself all the time. Some missionaries we met were so serious about saving the world that they were a general irritation to others. Others became emotionally unstable from keeping an intense "ought and should" mind in a culture whose national motto was "No Problem!" Sherry and I discovered that the way to survive emotionally on the missions field was to enjoy the perks each place offered. "Blessed are the flexible, they shall not break!" That became our motto. To keep our spirits up we began to explore the wonderful beaches that make Jamaica so famous.

On our anniversary, we decided to splurge and go to the exclusive Jamaica, Jamaica Resort in Runaway Bay. Our Jamaican resident's discount meant that we could go there as a couple for only $100 a day with room, all food and activities included. That was a lot of money to us, but it was our anniversary so we splurged.

We entered the lobby, all giggly with excitement, and took our bags to the room. Water has never been bluer than against the white beaches of Jamaica. We lazed around and eventually worked up a killer appetite for the all-you-can-eat seafood buffet. While savoring our lunch we saw a sign, "Scuba Lessons at the pool." Scuba, now that would be something to make this a special memory (anyway, it was also free).

Our instructor's name was Mike Young, a tall Chinese-Jamaican who had been trained by the SEALS of the Royal Navy. He was the perfect figure of a captain: tall, muscular, swaggering, loud and bold. Some ladies in the class cried when he scolded them for mistakes. Out they went! Rejected. No crybabies allowed. Some men couldn't take treading water for 5 minutes with a weight belt. No mercy! Scuba was a dangerous sport. Only the strong and totally obedient were allowed to participate. (We learned later that, in reality, Mike was only paid to take out one boatload. He had to find a way to reject the others somehow or take them at his own expense.) Sherry and I both like a challenge so we grunted it out and made the cut to do an introductory open water dive.

## *We Discover that Sailors Cuss*

While the boat ride made me queasy, and the act of pushing my face under water and sucking in a breath through
the regulator brought pure terror, my greatest source of
uneasiness was simply Mike and his friends. I am the
third generation of born-again Christians in my family. I
had been carefully shielded from the influences of the
world all my life. As a teen, I had entered into a drug-
using peer group and saw many horrible things, but I had
left all that behind six years ago and had served in the
ministry ever since. With Mike and company, I just did
not know how to respond. They looked me in the eyes
when they spoke, accepting me fully, assuming that I was
just like them. Then they told horribly crude jokes right in
front of my wife and looked our way, expecting us to be
dying with laughter like them. I couldn't believe they
would say such things in front of Sherry. Of course, they
celebrated the end of each safe dive with a round of beers.
They always offered us one in friendship. I was conflicted
inside. Do I laugh at their jokes to make them feel accepted or do I shake my head disapprovingly and say,
"Please don't say such things"? Do I accept the beer and
take a swig to be friendly, or do I say, "No thanks, I don't
drink alcohol" to demonstrate a higher standard of life so
they would ask if I was a Christian?

Sitting by the pool that day in this swirl of thoughts, the
Lord spoke to me. "You don't know how to live among ordinary people." I realized that my 25 years in a Christian
sub-culture had made the lives and ways of common people
a foreign thing to me. I could not name one lost person with
whom I had an ongoing friendship. I had not intentionally
eaten a meal with any lost person in many years. I was a pastor, trapped in my Christian world, salt trapped in the salt-

shaker. All my life as a believer I had wanted to make a difference in the lives of others, especially those who were lost, but I had never been able to. Now, I understood why.

I talked to Sherry about it on the way home. We determined to enter into an experiment. We would come to the coast twice a week and take diving lessons with Mike. We would just try to fit in the best we could. Love would show us the way.

## They Have Names

We discovered that lost people have names. There was Everett, Mike's dashing, sophisticated, muscular partner. "Mr. Pocket" was the dark silent mountain of a man who stayed in the background fixing things and looking for problems with groups under water before they became emergencies. His reactions saved many people from injuries.

His white pearly teeth would break through his dark face whenever you called to him. His words sounded like a song and his expressions always brought wisdom. And there was Mike's girlfriend who modeled swimsuits. They fought a lot, but they stayed together. We spent a lot of time with Mike's young assistant, Norman. Mike would yell at him sometimes to blow off steam, even if it seemed he didn't deserve it. There was also the pretty marine biologist who worked at the dive shop when school was on break and many others who came and went as the months passed.

All had hopes and dreams. All had burdens that they bore patiently as well as they could. All were trying to overcome their obstacles, deal with their own inner conflicts and live a happy life. They were caught in the spiral of their own habits and lifestyles and couldn't seem to get out, no matter how honestly they tried. The greatest surprise was Mike himself. In front of others he was on stage and felt he had to play the role of "Gruff Ol' Captain Mike," but when I sat all alone with him, he became boyish and humble, almost like I was his dad or a confessor priest. He knew his life wasn't right. He was a rascal, but he was so easy to love once you accepted him. He had a code of honor, a kind of ethic for his life that he lived up to by choice. One day he slid an envelope across a table to me. "Go buy some kid a pair of shoes so he can go to school, OK?" Then he walked away, embarrassed but probably elated at the same time.

We did not tell them that we were pastors initially. Sherry and I both hate that fake double standard of having people apologize to us for something they said because we are ministers. "Oh, sorry preacher, I didn't see you standing there." Ugh! With this group we were happy to see that, without carrying a Bible, or even "looking for a chance to witness" our influence began to grow in their lives. They instinctively started relating to us as pastoral figures, telling us things, looking for guidance, like we were the only two people they could talk to. They remarked about the stability of our lives and how in love we seemed. Years later, we came to understand that this was "spiritual authority," and that God had placed us over their lives for their good. For that period of time, He made them look up to us and listen to whatever we said because this was for their benefit. We thoroughly enjoyed our pastorate in Mandeville that year, but, to be honest, the most exciting thing that had ever happened to our lives as Christians was happening on Mondays with this authentic group of seeking sailors.

## A Tragedy Strikes

One day, with no warning, a friend walked into our home in the high country of Mandeville and said nonchalantly, "One of dem friends from de coast, him a dead. I heard it on de news jus nuh." No, it couldn't be! Who? Maybe another hotel. I called the resort's front desk in agony. "Was someone from the dive group killed?" I asked the man on the other end. "Yes, Mike Young is dead." He waited for a response from me, but I was so thunderstruck I couldn't reply. "Don't cry now!" he chided. But I did cry. I agonized and groaned and wept and grieved for weeks, and even until now. Mike was dead.

In typical Mike fashion, he had had a few drinks and had gotten in a car at night showing off and driving very fast. He had slammed into the back of a parked long-bed cargo truck that had no lights or reflectors. The police had then casually tossed his shattered, now-shrunken body into their trunk and drove it to the station, where his friends had to come and physically remove it and take it to an undertaker. Everyone was in shock.

The funeral was in Kingston at a Catholic Church. The priest assured everyone that Mike was in eternal bliss and that we could all go home in peace. Nobody believed the priest. One of his friends said, "If Mike heard that priest, I'm sure he was laughing his head off." We all went to a house to eat together. Sherry and I sat down and they all began to circle their chairs around us. We were their pastors now, whether they understood it or not. They sought our words to try and figure out this tragedy. We did the best we could.

We could have planted a church that day and probably would if we could do it over again. We moved from Jamaica shortly after that and started life over again in

Manila, planting a church out of people like the sailors who taught us to love the lost. We took with us the lessons we had learned about how to open our hearts to the lost in a natural flow of healthy, redemptive relationships. Through this lifestyle Lighthouse Christian Community was born. In the following chapters, we want to share some of the practical lessons we learned from interacting with our friends at Jamaica, Jamaica and here in Manila.

STEP ONE: Pray daily, "Lord, today, send me someone who needs your help."

# 6

# Pray This Prayer

## Just Do Four Things

Out of Mike's death we began to seek God for a way to become fruit-bearing Christians. We were broken at the death of this man whom we loved. He was the lost. We wanted to reach as many of them as we could before they, too, came to the end of their road.

God hears prayer. He showed us four simple things we could do each day that would make us a powerful influential force in the lives of others: pray to be used every day, tune into people, speak the name of Jesus with authority, and offer to pray on-the-spot for people who open up to us. These four things have changed our pattern of living from that day until now. Many people are now born-again and serving the Lord as a consequence of this simple revelation.

After moving to Manila to help establish a graduate school, we continued to practice these four things on a daily basis. It became the core of our missionary methodology. Through it we planted a church of 13 people in 1990. By its ninth birthday, that church had grown to 1,300 people.

The purpose of this book is to share these things with you. I hope you will purpose in your heart to put them into practice in your own lives. We hope that you will write us with stories of what God does through you as a result.

## The First Thing to Do:
## Pray This Prayer Every Day

The Bible is full of the recorded prayers of God's people. Some of these prayers became hymns for Israel or the early church (Psalms 23 and Mary's Magnificat are two examples). Some prayers are memorizable forms, to help us pray rightly (like the Lord's prayer).

Jesus taught us to pray in short, meaningful sentences. Some of the most powerful form prayers in the Bible are only one sentence long. One of these is found in the last words of the Book of the Revelation: "*Amen. Even so, come, Lord Jesus.*" (Rev. 22:20 KJV)

I think this little one is a jewel. My favorite part is "even so." I can remember being a teenager trying to serve the Lord. I didn't want the Kingdom to come until I could get out of the house and become an adult. Then I moved out and went to college. Now, I didn't want Jesus to come until I had gotten married. Then I got married and I really hoped the rapture could be delayed long enough for us to have a child, etc., etc.

This little prayer is given to guide our hearts into having proper affections regarding the things of his earthly life. It is important to pray this prayer every day, no matter what our inner longings are. It should be prayed something like this, "Lord, I know there's no sex in heaven and I really want to know what it's like, and Lord, I'd really like to be married and see my children, and Lord, I have dreams for a house I'll build myself, and a career plan that will make me a giant in the business world and show everyone how talented you have made me, but EVEN SO, come Lord Jesus." That's good praying.

Jesus had a similar prayer that he used to keep his heart aligned with the purposes of God. It went, "*Nevertheless, not my will, but yours be done."*(Luke 22:42) In his most agonizing moment in the garden, when his natural human will was wrestling with the demands of Calvary, he used this prayer to make sure that he was properly submitted to the purposes and will of the Father.

Our first revelation from God was a prayer to pray daily: *"Lord, send me someone today who needs your help."* Like the other two prayers I mentioned, it is supposed to be prayed even when it is the exact opposite of your human mind's desires. It is like a drag anchor for a ship being thrown about by the contrary currents. It forces us to line up and face forward. It keeps us from being blown off course like so many other ships.

I began to pray this little prayer, *"Lord, send me today someone who needs your help."* Most days I still don't want to pray it. I am a focused person. I like a planned day and when it is interrupted and my schedule is thrown off, it takes grace to accept it cheerfully. But I still pray the prayer. I have to pray it so that I will love what God loves. He may have a 911 call for me today that is more important than the dozens of urgent things I have created.

## *"Lord, Send Someone to Me"*

This part of the prayer actually lets me off the hook a bit. When I was a very young Christian I came to understand my duty to win the lost before they died and went to Hell. I became so obsessed with the fate of the lost that I pressured myself to do things that were so unnatural for me. One night, for example, I sat outside the house of a neighbor I didn't know and agonized for over an hour on whether I was supposed to knock on his door and witness to him. I didn't do it and I felt horrible. I went back the next day and struck up a conversation, trying to lead into the big sermon I had to deliver to him. It was a disaster.

He was totally bewildered by me and I was shaking and sweating all over. This prayer, "send them to me" delivers me from ever facing that fate again (I score 70% on the introversion scale).

I read the great commission, from Matthew 28, in the Greek (that's the benefit of a seminary education). It has only one verb (μαθητευσατε), "make disciples." The word "go" as used in that passage isn't a verb; it's a participle. It is better translated, "in your going make disciples." This says to me that the calling on most believers is to simply go about their ordinary day keeping their eyes open for the lost. God will do the rest. That's what I do now.

God has strategically placed you in the workplace, school, and neighborhood that is perfectly suited for the mission he will send you on each day. Whether you know it or not, you will use the divinely ordained laundry mat and shop at the specific grocery He has led you to. Philippians 2:13 says, "For it is God who works in you to will and to act according to his good purpose." It probably isn't necessary for most of us to knock on the doors of strangers. Just make friends with people when you naturally meet them along your journey and pursue their friendship in natural ways. God will work out all the coincidences so that you will meet them when they are ready.

This readiness, unfortunately, isn't usually bilateral. God has to focus on when *they* are ready and trust that we, as his servants, will respond to the need when we see it, no matter how busy we have scheduled ourselves to be. Death to self is the beginning of life in Christ. You will never walk the deeper path with God until you are willing to sacrifice what you want to obey what He wants.

The prayer, *"Lord, today, send me someone who needs your help,"* is your declaration of love for the Father. Romans 12:2

says, "Present yourselves as a living sacrifice." Then Paul adds, "*This* is true worship." It's easy to clap hands or sing along with a choir. Real worship is laying your will on the altar and saying, "Lord let your kingdom come, and mine go. Let your will be done regardless of my personal appetites." What does God will? The salvation of the lost. He wants his lost children rescued. He will position you properly if you will agree to embrace the mission and do it with all your heart.

"Lord, today, send me someone who needs your help." This prayer keeps us focused on spending time only with those who are already needing help. Get past the fear that you will have to force your way into the lives of closed people. There are millions of people out there today who are on the verge of a major spiritual breakthrough or a major personal collapse, depending upon whether any of us get to them or not.

## Everybody Has Some Horrible Days

In the second year of our marriage, we set our hearts on moving to Colorado and helping to plant churches there. Colorado had always been our dream. Sherry had tried to go there as a counselor for a summer camp years before. My dad had taken me and my two brothers to a dude ranch when I was 18 and I have been a Willie Nelson fan ever since.

In our last semester of graduate school, Sherry and I were invited by a church in Colorado to interview for a position with their youth as a starting place for a life there. We flew in, spent days socializing, and even went skiing with some of the church families. We got close with other young couples and lay awake at night talking about who we liked already and why. We stayed in the house where they said we would live and shoveled the snow off the driveway.

We liked the pastor and he seemed to like us too. I bought a pair of skis that were on sale. We called our parents from there and shared our excitement. Someone even suggested that we just leave our skis and suitcases there since we would be returning in just a few months.

We flew home and continued to dream of life out west. I watched the Denver Broncos with renewed enthusiasm, although they were already my favorite team. I waited for a week for the final thumbs up and the date on which they would be expecting us. Two weeks went by, then six, then eight. One day, just before chapel, Dr. Crick, my mentor and placement director, called me into his office. "I finally called the pastor myself today, Chuck. He doesn't want you." There were no reasons given. After nearly 20 years, I still don't know what happened.

I am not a terribly emotional person, but that day, as a 22-year-old kid, I was crushed beyond words. All I could think was, "How will I tell this to Sherry?" I felt rejected and abandoned, and that I had failed on my first attempt at leading us into our family's future. I went into the empty chapel alone, lay across the altar and just quietly wept. In a while, the crowd came in for chapel and a few noticed me there. At that moment, I didn't want counseling. I didn't want a pep talk. I didn't want to read a helpful book. I just wanted someone to put his arm around me and either pray for me or at least sit there with me. I felt so alone. A student with whom I hadn't really interacted very much knelt beside me, put his arm around me and prayed for me quietly. When I was tired, we sat down and he took his wallet and opened it. He was a married man with two kids. His opened wallet had only a five-dollar bill inside. He took it out and handed it to me. I couldn't take it. He told me not to be proud, but to let him do what the Lord had told him to do as an encouragement to me.

I have hardly seen Chris Swift since that day. He lives in Holland and I in the Philippines, but whenever I see his name in a missions publication or run into him about every 10 years or so, I love him all over again. I think about what he did for me that day. It was just right. On time. Just what I needed. I try to be that kind of help to others.

## The Day That Matters Most

Surely you have had days like that, probably not a dozen of them over your entire lifetime, but each one significant beyond their short duration. Maybe someone was there for you. Doubtless, sometimes they were not. That's what the prayer is all about. It is designed to align us to be what the world needs us to be: the person who is there for others on the one day that matters most. On that day they will be ready and open to be ministered to by Him. In this little prayer, "Lord, today, send me someone who needs your help" we ask God to channel in our direction, the flow of people having "one of those days" so we can be the one who truly sees them and reaches out in time.

"I was naked and you clothed me, sick and in prison and you visited me." That's what Jesus said. If you read the passage you will find that there will be a crowd of people at the judgment who will be shocked that they are given such a prominent reception and placement in heaven's society. "Lord, why?" they will ask. "You were there for me when I needed you" will answer.

Go to work with God today. Pray this prayer, "Lord, send me today someone who needs your help."

STEP TWO: Tune-in to Other People

# 7

# Tune-in to Others

*I* heard a story a few years ago about a man traveling on an airplane with a little girl. The child cried and fretted for a long time and the other passengers were becoming irate. The little three-year-old just kept crying, "I want to ride in the back with Mommy!" Finally, the lady behind the man could take no more. She leaned over and scolded him about the need to control his "kid." She told him that it was rude to bring children on the plane if he couldn't guarantee that they would be quiet and re-spect the rights of the other passengers. She told him that she was fed up with the crying and that she had paid good money for this flight. "For heaven's sake, just let her go to her mother!" she demanded. The man spoke in a soft voice, apologizing for the inconvenience. "The problem is that my wife was killed yesterday morning in an accident and we are taking her body to her family's hometown for the funeral. Sarah doesn't understand how we can let Mommy ride alone back there. She was always scared to fly and asked Sarah to hold her hand. I'm very sorry for her cry-ing. She's just worried about her mom. I'll try to keep her more quiet."

Many of us have had similarly embarrassing experiences. The lady probably felt ashamed for her selfishness after that encounter. You just never know what baggage other people are carrying at any given time. If you truly want to be a soul winner you must pray about it daily, then do a second thing: tune-in to other people.

Everyone has his or her own interests and preoccupations. In a mall, my daughter, Kristin, instinctively sees the girl with the triple pierced ears or purple hair. "Wow! Soooo cool!" Sherry instantly zooms in on pieces of pottery or old furniture. I, meanwhile, see any new technology. (On the other hand, I am totally blind to draperies, upholstery, and ladies shoes.) It is human nature to be attentive to your own moods and desires. Soul winners grow past this. They choose to "tune-in" to other people. They listen carefully to others, noting emotion in their voice and their hidden cries for help. They start each day with the prayer, "Father, send me someone today who needs your help." Then they go into their day with their radar on, searching for that person sent by God.

## When Jesus Came to Applebee's

A few years ago we were at an Applebee's restaurant and had possibly the worst waitress we have ever had. She was totally distracted, although the place was half-empty. She got the order messed up. She never returned after bringing the food. We had to wave wildly to try to attract her attention when the drinks ran low. If we asked two or three times, she might remember to bring the ketchup. It was frustrating. Naturally, we wanted to express our dissatisfaction with her poor performance (If you pay $15 for ribs you want to enjoy the experience, right?). Fortunately, Sherry was yielded enough to the Holy Spirit to take the harried girl by the hand, look into her eyes and say, "I think you are having a tough day." The girl burst into tears and began pouring her heart out. It was a sad story, and before long she realized that this wasn't appropriate behavior for a waitress in the middle of the restaurant. "Will you wait for me, please? I get off in ten minutes." She was pleading. I waited in the car for an hour while Sherry held the sobbing waitress in the ladies room and heard all the details of just how messed up a young life can become. Jesus had come to Applebee's to introduce himself to this young lady. He came in the face of Sherry.

We could have easily missed the opportunity to reach out to this hurting young lady, but for the second step, "Tune-in to other people." Mind you, this takes a daily discipline, but it is a skill that can be mastered by anyone who has a heart to learn it. "Everyone should be quick to listen. Slow to speak. Slow to become angry." (James 1:19 NIV) I think we would win the world a lot faster if we would quit talking at people so much and start listening to their hearts more. Jesus said, "Out of the overflow of the heart the mouth speaks." This means that I will never understand the truth about another person until I get them to talk about themselves.

### People like to talk about themselves

People like to talk about themselves if anyone will just listen. I once listened to a set of tapes on the art of negotiating produced by a man named Roger Dawson. In them he tells the story of a game he used to play when he was in real estate sales. He and a trainee would knock on doors and see how much information they could gather from the homeowner. The trainee would try first and get a little information. Roger would take the next house. "Hello, I'm Roger Dawson, a real estate broker, and we were driving by and noticed this beautiful home. Did you build it yourself? It must have cost a fortune; do you mind telling us how much it cost you to build? Wow! What a great deal! Your husband must be a builder, right? An accountant! With a home like this he would have to be in the income bracket of, say, over $100,000. Oh, $75,000. Well, he's a great money manager to afford such a house. What kind of deal did he get on the interest? What bank was that? etc., etc. He would sometimes walk away with twenty pieces of incredibly sensitive information. Why? He asked follow up questions in a non-threatening way and showed interest and honor toward the other person.

How many times have you asked, "How's it going?" only to have the person say "Fine," but with hesitation in their voice? That hesitation, to someone who listens, is like a flag waving the words, "Please ask me more!" In our day, everyone is so hurried and busy that they seldom follow up on such obvious cries for help, even if they notice them. Soul winners understand that they are on a divine mission. God will lead them to people in need of His help. Soul winners pay attention to the people they meet all day long, listening for the one with a burden or a trial.

## People Hide Their Hurts

One of the characteristics of the human race is our tendency to be hypocrites, pretending to be something better than we really are. After twenty-five years of life, we are practically masters at hiding the truth about ourselves unless life's circumstances overwhelm us like a tidal wave. So, don't think that the drunk in the gutter is necessarily the one crying for help. It might just as well be the businessman next to you on the plane whose wife has just left him. Their relationship has been stormy for years. Last week, she left and took the precious children that he loves and lives for each day. She is angry and is telling them horrible secret things about him. Now he can't see them. She will probably marry someone else within a year, and his darling daughters will end up calling that man "Dad." He hasn't slept more than three hours any night this week. He groans in silent agony even as he thumbs casually through his magazine on the plane.

I've quit asking people, "How are you?" because they don't even hear it as a true inquiry. Now I ask, "How is your life?" and they almost always pause, think, and give me some kind of substantial reply. Sometimes, they happily share about their good fortune. At other times they realize that I really care and so they share their latest dilemma and sometimes, their pain.

## God Will Draw Them to You if You Will Tune in to Them

Sherry and I have been on this journey into the harvest field over the last sixteen years. Over time, we have found ourselves becoming more and more attractive to others. Before, people just passed me by and I never noticed. I was glad to be left alone. I had a handful of friends and that was enough for me. All that changed as I gradually began to tune into others. Giving people the gift of attention made them feel loved and honored. They began to be magnetically drawn to us, not just the emotionally shattered people, but also all kinds of people who were in some way or other searching for a higher meaning in their lives.

We have learned to be sensitive to the "coincidences" of the Holy Spirit. If I help someone in the grocery store reach for a box on the top shelf and then meet the same person again at the McDonald's playground while we both watch our five-year-olds play, then I assume this must be a God-thing. So I pay attention. Ask their name. Swap phone numbers and most importantly begin praying for them. Then, Sherry and I "pursue" their friendship, knowing that there must be a reason God is causing our paths to cross. A cookout at our house on a Saturday will usually reveal why.

## What Should I Say?

Sherry and I have gradually learned not to "talk at people for Jesus." Dietrich Bonhoeffer, a pastor executed by the Nazis, said that the only way for the church to win the modern, secular world is to shut up. Quit the endless "God talk." Stop "witnessing" and start listening to the people of the world. Pay attention to their world and show love and practical concern. He said that if all the churches in the world would just do that, we could re-establish the credibility of Christianity in its religion-less form within a generation. Then we could again preach the word of God in its original power. I think he has it about right. It seems that many would-be evangelists fish for men with a treble hook (the one with three hooks) and no bait. They just want to thrash about in the sea of humanity hoping to snag some souls for Christ. Whether they hook them in the eye, the gill or the fin is of no matter.

The Bible says, "Taste and see that the Lord is good." Everyone deserves to "taste" Christ for themselves and make up their own minds whether to be his disciple or not. Our job is to genuinely, with no fleshly motive, tune into people. As they say, "They will never care how much you know until they know how much you care."

## Divine Authority

If you will determine to become God's face of love and encouragement to a dying world, God will give you the powerful gift of divine authority. You will become "bigger than life" to the ones God will draw to you. They will not be able to see your weaknesses and failings (at least for a time). They will see you as a person who has it all together. They will want whatever it is that you have. Water flows downhill. People have to look up to you in order to listen to you and drink the "water of life" the Lord will give them through you. It is a powerful gift and I have been amazed at it since I noticed it. As a young seeker I, too, followed my spiritual heroes because of this divine anointing. I still honor and respect each of them for what they contributed to my life.

As you begin to build relationships with the seekers God brings into your life, please remember to treat this gift of authority with the sacredness it deserves. I once watched God open a door into the life of a leader in a third world nation. This man was a billionaire. His money made him politically powerful. Many of the streets in the capital city were named after his family. I became marginally connected to him through a friendship between my six-year-old son and his grandson. We planted a church and his daughter-in-law began to attend regularly. Everyone saw the changes God worked in her life. We prayed and worked for months to build relationships that could allow us to speak with authority to all the members of this spiritually needy family. Then tragedy struck. The man was paralyzed from the neck down in a freak accident. His family began to seek for help from many sources. A friend of mine went boldly to the home and was led into the man's own bedroom (something never done in this culture). My friend laid his hands on the distraught man and prayed for healing. He led him to pray to receive Christ as Lord—and then he asked him for material help on a business matter. This family's open, sincere heart slammed shut instantly. He was hurt and felt used. To this day, I still agonize over this horrible loss.

You can count on it. God will give you favor with the lost and you will become an important figure in their lives because this is necessary to their being able to receive the good news about salvation. Don't ever abuse this sacred trust. Be careful of your own life's inconsistencies. Allow the pressure of being watched by these "babies" to force you into a deeper life of integrity.

I love Isaiah 50:4:"the Sovereign Lord has given me an instructed tongue, to know the word that sustains the weary. He wakens me morning by morning, wakens my ear to listen like one being taught. The Sovereign Lord has opened my ears. . . ." Can you see the gift God gave Isaiah? He learned to give the gift of time and attention. He learned (it takes practice) to listen long and then speak powerful words of encouragement and life to discouraged, weary people. Why not stop right now and ask God to open your ears so you can hear the cries of the hurting? Then begin to practice "tuning-in" today.

**STEP THREE: Declare the Name of Jesus**

# 8

# Say the
# Name of Jesus

*I* grew up knowing about the power of Jesus, but it wasn't until the summer of 1980 that I realized how mighty it is to simply say that name. I was twenty-one and working a summer job as a maintenance helper at Electromagnetic Sciences in Norcross, GA. I enjoyed the job and learned quite a bit about painting, plumbing and doing electrical work (getting electrocuted once in the process). I tried to be friendly and represent the Lord as well as I could in that company. All summer long, I had the same conversations. After introducing myself to the people I met, we would eventually chat and begin sharing a bit of information about ourselves. When they asked about me, I would always say that I was studying for the ministry. Most times they would counter with, "How did that happen?" That was my cue to begin to share what Christ had done for me.

One day at lunch, dozens of people were buzzing in conversation, eating sandwiches and joking around. My lunch mate asked that magic question and I began to give my reply. In a normal voice I said, "Well, Jesus changed my life completely." I wish you could have seen the impact that the word "Jesus" had on the room. Do you remember the E. F. Hutton commercials of the 80's? The same thing happened. The entire room hushed. Heads turned and looked at me. I, of course, stood on the table and preached to the crowd and everyone got saved. I wish! In reality, I blushed every shade of red and froze up completely until other conversations resumed and the spotlight was off of me. Then I continued to share with the person I was talking to.

I left the plant that day feeling ashamed that I hadn't had more boldness, but also amazed at what had happened when I said the name of Jesus with reverence in the presence of others who whose lifestyles demonstrated that they didn't believe in him or follow him as Lord.

Philippians chapter two says that God has given Jesus the name above all names and that every knee in heaven and on earth will bow to the sound of that name. When we say that name a spiritual war ensues. The forces of heaven fight for the glory of that name and the Savior it represents. The forces of darkness do everything they can to keep men and women from bowing their knees to Christ and accepting his lordship. Anytime the name of Jesus is proclaimed, it is a spiritually significant event.

Christianity is not so much a religion about God in general as it is about Christ in particular. We are the disciples of a man named Jesus who was born 2,000 years ago in the Middle East. We proclaim that he was, in fact, the Almighty Creator God, clothed in flesh and participating in full humanity for our salvation. We believe that his death is the central event in human history, and that he was resurrected from death, never to die again. We teach that through his resurrection he gained power over Satan and sin for every person who will ever be born. All of the sins of humanity have been forgiven by his sacrifice on our behalf. Through him, we gain new birth into an eternal life that begins now. We will live the rest of our earthly lives animated and guided by his own Spirit that now dwells within our bodies. This same Spirit will raise us from the dead or will rapture us immediately into his presence when his Kingdom comes. That is an amazing testimony! It is the gospel.

You simply cannot proclaim the gospel without using the name, Jesus. You can't just say "God," "Lord," or "the Big Man Upstairs." You have to say, "Jesus." I have found a natural hesitation, even in myself, to saying the name of Jesus in a conversation. You can say "God" and "the Lord" and nobody raises an eyebrow. But when you say the name, Jesus, you get the reaction I described above. Something happens. That "something" has both positive and negative aspects.

Saying the name of "Jesus" identifies you as a follower of Christ, a "Jesus Freak" to those who are hostile to Christ. You never hear anyone in the media bash Buddha or mock Mohammed. Jesus, on the other hand, gets attacked every day. Preachers are lampooned on sitcoms. Sincere testimonies about the amazing transformations Christ has made in people's lives are pushed aside as evidence of emotional instability. Jesus said that the student is not above his master. "If they persecute me, they will persecute you also." (John 15:20)

The early Christians learned to boldly proclaim the name of Jesus and to rejoice when they were counted worthy to suffer for the name. We have to reclaim that same spirit to survive spiritually in these last days. If Jesus is our Savior, then we must not be ashamed of him in front of our wicked and godless generation. When we get a chance to "brag on Jesus" we must use that precious opportunity without fear and shyness. Beloved, we must not be ashamed of Jesus. He died for us when we were still his enemies. He is, in truth, the Lord of Glory and we should boldly declare our confidence in him to everyone we can.

## Saying Jesus' Name also Releases Power from Heaven

Although they knew it might invite persecution, the early church didn't hesitate to declare Christ by name because of the amazing, positive things that happen whenever you say the name of Jesus. Blind eyes are opened. The deaf hear. The depressed are set at liberty. Most importantly, the lost are found and brought home to the Father. When a believer, any believer, speaks to a lost person in compassion and boldly declares Jesus as the answer to their search, you just never know what incredible things might happen!

Peter learned that 3,000 people could get saved all at once. He also learned that Christ could redeem an entire extended family and fill them all with the Holy Spirit in an instant. Philip learned that a powerful government leader could become instantly convicted about his sins and wish to be baptized and take the gospel to his nation. Paul learned repeatedly that pagans, with no knowledge of the scriptures whatsoever, could be overwhelmed by the power of the Holy Spirit, fall on their knees and embrace Jesus—all because someone dared to say his name to them.

One of the most famous stories in the missions organization we serve under is that of a mountain tribe in Latin America that worshipped the gods of nature. A pastor living on the plains received instruction from the Lord that he had to hike deep into the dangerous, distant mountains to preach the gospel where these people lived. He obeyed and began the arduous journey, along with his pregnant wife and small child. Eventually, he located a village and entered it, preaching the gospel and healing the sick. When he declared that the Savior's name was Jesus, the people all began to weep. Everyone turned to the Lord! They later explained that they had received a previous revelation in their dreams that the "God above all gods" would send someone to tell them His name. This precious child of God had the honor of being that messenger.

The third step in effectively evangelizing those who open up to you is to simply introduce the name of Jesus into the conversation. You will know that it is time to do this whenever anyone opens their heart and tells you about their personal struggles and burdens. At that moment you must walk through the open door they are holding and let them know that Jesus is the answer to their problems. The angels are waiting for that cue.

## Brag on Jesus!

Learn to find joy in bragging on Jesus! Tell them what he has done for you. Tell them what he has done for others with similar conditions. Preach Christ boldly and feel the power of the Holy Spirit welling up within you. Look them in the eyes. Let God use you. Don't talk about your church, or your great pastor. Don't invite them to join the softball team or offer a counseling book. Tell them about Jesus Christ, the Son of God who died for them! Make them read Jeremiah 29:11–12. (You should memorize this passage. I find that it is the most powerful first thought to place in the mind of a seeker.) Help them see the truth of John 10:10, that the devil has plans to destroy everything of beauty in their lives, and that Christ has come to give them an incredibly wonderful experience of life.

I don't make promises regarding their problems being resolved in the way they think they ought to be. God knows what is best. He will do what He needs to. Our human duty is to bow and become humble before Him or we cannot know Him at all. Let God be God! I can't promise that God will make her husband love her again, or that their home won't be foreclosed on this Monday as planned. I *can* say that if they will fully surrender their life and will to Jesus, God has a big master plan that will lead them to a wonderful life and that one day this problem will seem a small thing because their life will be so victorious and happy. Who they are is more important than what they do or own. I can promise them on the authority of God's word, that if they will surrender to Christ, completely and totally, their life will operate in a positive upward path.

In these first, crucial moments with the seeker, we must keep the focus on the "meeting" they now need to have with Jesus. Even to talk about "God," I think, opens the door to spiritual confusion. People these days worship all kinds of gods and lords. Our Father God will do miracles for them, but only to testify to the truth about Jesus. He wants the world to know Christ and to recognize his sacrifice for their sins so that they can appropriate the blessings of the covenant for themselves.

After praying for God to send us someone who needs His help, we tune into other people. Someone along the way will open up to us. That's our divine appointment. We listen carefully to their story. Then, after we understand them and their heart, we begin to speak about Jesus. That's the third step. Do this and watch the power of the name of Jesus being released in your personal soul-winning ministry at school, work or in your own home.

**STEP FOUR: Offer to Pray For Them**

# 9

# Pray with People on the Spot

*T*he fourth step in our simple evangelism methodology is perhaps the hardest to many people: offer to pray with them on the spot. "Can't I just say, 'I'll pray for you?'" Nope. I'll tell you why. There are basically two reasons. The first is that if you get into the habit of saying this to people constantly you may well forget it entirely before you even get home. The second reason is much more important. It's about them. It is important to God's purpose in their life that they attach the miracle they are about to receive to the time the disciple of Jesus prayed for them. If you just walk away with the well wishing "I'll pray for you" and they do get a breakthrough, they may not connect the event directly to an encounter with Jesus Christ. They may think "Wow! The crystal I just bought really works!" unless you make a point to stop and pray personally with them on behalf of Jesus.

## My Jewish Neighbor

The first time God brought this home to me was with my neighbor in Jamaica, a man named David. David and his wife were from Israel. They were in Jamaica on contract to demonstrate the amazing Israeli farming techniques in strawberry production at a nearby agricultural research center. He was, like most Jews I have met from Israel, sadly empty of any meaningful sense of God in his life. "Maybe there's a God, maybe not; either way this doesn't have any connection to me," was his attitude. One weekend, while they were out, his house was burglarized. Sherry and I went next door to sympathize. We tried to develop a friendship with him and his wife as best we could, waiting for the Lord to open the door into their hearts.

Then David hurt his back. He damaged it so badly that he was in constant pain. We didn't learn of it until the night before he was set to return to Tel Aviv for surgery. I summoned my courage and went to his door. "David, can I pray for you?" I asked. He nodded, but didn't even open the iron gate to his porch. I reached my hand inside the grill and laid it gently on his back. I just prayed a simple prayer that ended with, "Lord Jesus, please heal David to show him that you are real and that you have a plan for his life. Amen." Then Sherry and I smiled, left, went home and *really* prayed.

Ten days later David was back. It seems that while on the plane he felt something warm moving through his back. By the time he landed in Israel he had no pain at all. He went to the surgeon (who said there was now nothing wrong at all), had a short vacation, and returned to work. It was just a seed, but an important event in his spiritual journey—a confrontation with the truth about Jesus, the Messiah.

## Everyone Gets One Miracle

Hebrews 2:4 says that whenever the message of Jesus is proclaimed, God himself will bear witness with miracles, signs and wonders. The prayer warriors in our Jamaican church held to the belief that everyone in the world was entitled to one miracle each, in order to demonstrate that the gospel isn't just a made-up story from an old book of folklore. If Jesus is alive and is the master of death, disease and Hell itself, then he and his Church ought to be able to prove it.

Most Christians have little experience in working miracles. That's because they almost never pray with anyone— except other believers, and then, mostly in church. Read the gospels. Most miracles were for unbelievers. One of the characteristic sayings of the Gospel of John is "after the miracle he believed. . . ." Jesus was a wonder-worker in his earthly life. Today, in his wider global ministry through his people, Jesus is still busy saving, healing and bringing deliverance to thousands every day. He said that after he went to the Father he would send the Spirit upon us and that we would do greater works than he had done in his earthly days (John 14:12–13). His plan is that ordinary disciples will go out into their daily routines and, upon encountering people in need, simply testify about the power of Jesus, lay hands on that person and pray for a sign.

The reason most of us see so few true miracles is that, again, we reserve our prayer for believers, and in church. If you will begin praying for the sick, depressed and hurting people God sends right to you, you will begin to see the miraculous work of God in your personal ministry at work, in the neighborhood and on campus. One of the greatest joys of my life is to pray with people for their needs. It's a no-lose situation. If they get the expected miracle, then— Hallelujah! They have encountered the miraculous power of God. If they don't get the situation fixed exactly as they originally hoped, then, at least they met this really special, loving person who held their hands, prayed with them sincerely, and called them up later in the week to see how they were doing. Either way they will know that God knows them and has a plan for their lives. Either way, they have received a valid witness of the reality of Jesus.

It all boils down to your willingness to be crucified to yourself so that you can serve God. Entering into the praying-for-people ministry will definitely separate you from the crowd. You don't have to be loud, showy or obnoxious. True people of prayer are never like that anyway. You do have to be willing to stop being you as a person and start being the "servant and messenger of God" instead. As persons, we are all concerned with how we look in public. Is my hair fixed right? How do others perceive me? Servants of God care about the Master's wishes. Did the Master receive what He was hoping for? Has anyone represented Jesus to this girl he is trying to speak to?

## Like an Angel

In the Bible, we have many stories about the day when an angel appeared to someone or other. It is always the same type of story. A person is having a genuine crisis. In agony, they cry out to God. Then one day—Whammo! Out of the blue, an angel appears with a message from God. Whether it is Abraham, Zechariah, Manoah or Gideon, the person begins to date their entire life story by that event. "OK, there was my life before the angel came and then there is my new promise-filled life after the angel came with the message from God." Angels stimulate faith and bring out the best side in the persons they confront or comfort.

When we follow the simple four-step approach to living that we have been describing, we take up the ministry of the angels. Meeting us becomes an extraordinary experience people go home and talk about. "Honey, you wouldn't believe what happened to me today! I was at lunch with this lady I just met, and, well, I don't really know why I told her, but it just poured out. I told her how we have been trying to have a baby for five years now, and, do you know what she did? She looked me in the eyes and said, "God loves you and has a plan to bless your life." Then she took my hand and prayed for me to have a baby boy. Isn't that amazing!" What is happening in this story? Faith is being stimulated by the unusual event of a messenger (that's what the word angel means anyway) from God who came and gave someone special attention.

## But I'm Shy

I was in Florida once and had a man approach me after the service. He was excited about knowing the Lord and wanted so badly to tell me how it happened. Here's his story:

> I had an infection in my foot that had gone inside and spread. It became unbearably painful.

I groaned in agony and lost all appetite. When I finally went to the doctor, he said, "I'm sorry, but gangrene is setting in. Your foot is going to have to come off." They scheduled the surgery for Monday. On Sunday, I was at home, depressed and in pain. A man from work came by, knocked on the door, and they let him in to see me. He greeted me, said he was sorry to hear about my situation and asked if he could pray for me. I said, "Sure."

He bowed his head, put his hand gently on my leg and prayed so quietly that I couldn't even make out what he said. Then he got up and said that he was going to church and that they would all pray for me and that he would check on me after service again.

As soon as he left, I felt a heat in my leg. I pulled the covers off and watched, in amazement, as the bright red infected streaks that had climbed up my leg in the last day or two began to retreat toward the knee, then to the calf, ankle and into my toe. My toe became bright red and purple, then the skin burst open and awful corruption began to seep out. I went to the bathroom, showered and just kept feeling better. For the first time in weeks I could put my weight on the foot. I went to the kitchen and began to fix myself something to eat. After a while, my friend returned, looked in the kitchen door and smiled at me. I still have my leg (*to illustrate, he bounced on it a few times*) and I've been walking with Jesus ever since.

Notice what is missing from the story: we see no rip-snorting evangelist, no loud prayers, no pressure. Not even one pastor was involved. Here is just an ordinary

Christian guy, a guy so shy that he doesn't even pray out loud. I think that God is in heaven with a lightening bolt of miraculous power, ready to encounter and reveal Himself to a spiritually lost child within the path you will travel today. He wants to reveal himself to them so badly and is ready—if he can just find someone to lay hands on them. You see, God seldom does anything without a human partner. That's what Romans 10:14 is all about: "Everyone who calls on the name of the Lord will be saved . . . but how can they believe without someone to proclaim Christ to them?" Lost people stay lost until someone represents Jesus in person. Some person has to come to them and be the human conduit for the Holy Spirit to flow through from the spirit-world to the natural one. Can you conceive of yourself becoming even an "empty straw" for God? That shouldn't take much faith.

## Ron Kenoly Laid Hands on Me

In the mid 90's, the Lord used Ron Kenoly in a powerful way in the Philippines. It was right after his "Lift Him Up!" album ignited praise and worship around the globe. Churches everywhere began to experience a freedom and exuberance through the songs on that album and the others he released around that time. Sherry and I had been in the process of planting and strengthening Lighthouse Christian Community for about four years. One area where we had always struggled was in our music. We just didn't have many musicians. Our singing was half-hearted. We all wanted things to improve, but didn't really know how. In addition to church planting, I was also working full-time to establish a new graduate program to train leaders at the Asian Seminary of Christian Ministries in downtown Makati. My emotional, physical and spiritual reserves were just about shot. I was developing nervous twitches in my right eye. I was tired and wanted so desperately to be refreshed and released into a new depth of worship.

Right on time, Ron Kenoly came to the Philippines and rocked the house. We took everyone we could from the church. What a time of joy and release! During the concert, frantic engineers came to tell us that we had to stop worshipping so freely in the conference center because the entire balcony was flexing like a trampoline. They feared it might collapse under the "standing room only" weight and kill everyone below. We praised the Lord anyhow (but bounced less) and began to believe that we could become a worshipping church after all.

The next afternoon Ron had an invitation-only meeting for local pastors. I was blessed with an invitation and took my place in the small auditorium, about ten rows back. He mostly sang his new songs and talked about how pastors and worship leaders could flow together in ministry, so that their churches could enjoy greater liberty in the Lord and access the flowing anointing of the Holy Spirit. Then he began to describe spiritual dryness, the bone-weariness that a good person can get from exhausting himself in ministry. He described times of tiredness in his own life when he craved the presence of the Lord, cried out to God and was refreshed. He couldn't have described me more perfectly at that moment. He asked anyone who needed a refreshing to come to the front. About a hundred of us lined up. We began to sing, "Anointing . . . fall on me!" I raised my hands and began to sense the warm, familiar presence of the Holy Spirit mending me. I was so full of faith and earnest desire for God that there was an almost tangible electricity around and through me, sort of like a static electricity build up.

It seemed like a long time before Bro. Ron made it across the room to our side. I remember thinking, "I am so charged and ready for God to move that *anybody* could touch me now and I'd be refilled." As I mused on this, I imagined the janitor mopping the floor, and seeing Ron overwhelmed with the altar response, just reaching across and touching people. I knew that if any believer had done so, I would have experienced a total release of the Holy Spirit within me.

In that altar, God helped me to understand the secret of helping people receive supernatural infillings from the Lord. (Up to that time I had worked earnestly trying to become a "supercharged battery" of anointing from my own devotional practice and sincere efforts to be a man of faith and integrity. I wanted so desperately to "bring" blessing to the hurting people I met.) Now that I was the one in need, I could understand the process better. It's all about timing. If a seeking person is reached on the right day, his need and faith arise to secure a powerful outpouring upon him. The encounter God has ordained between us builds a bond and the anointing of the Spirit begins to flow already. My role is to bring them into a supernatural encounter with God Himself, by building their faith and expectation. If my obedience has been instant and natural, then I will have entered their life at the moment of their need. Basically anyone in Christ can pray any kind of faithful prayer at that point and God will act in power because the one in need is primed to receive.

Only in heaven will I know how many times Sherry and I have prayed with other people. It has become a routine joy in our lives. Our experience is that the power of God released in such moments increases through time as you exercise your faith, and continually practice this basic ministry activity. I am a quiet person by nature and am often amazed at the testimonies of those we pray for. They often have powerful experiences, as anointing flows from the Lord, even in those times when I do not feel a thing. The point is, it's about them, not us. God has a meeting arranged with them and has been preparing them to receive His visit for months or even years. We just have to show up for work and do our job so the encounter can happen.

## *Let's Review*

Let's review the four steps again. In order to become a fruit-bearing person, we covenant with God to do the following:

1. **Pray every morning:** "Lord, send me someone today who needs your help."
2. **Tune into others:** ask follow-up questions, listen carefully. Someone will tell you about a personal problem. That's your green light.
3. **Brag on Jesus:** tell them what he has done for you and for others. Tell them that he loves them and has a plan for their life and wants to reveal himself to them to prove he's real.
4. **Offer to pray for them on the spot:** this fixes it in their mind as an unusual God-event, and provides a chance for God's power to flow into them.

I encourage you to pray for anyone who shares a problem with you. Pray in a private place, in a normal voice, briefly and with complete sincerity. Try to follow up with them, if possible, and give them your card so they can call you if they need you. Please do not see this as the end of your work in their lives. It only opens the door and earns you the right to speak into their lives in the future, as you now begin to guide them on to right paths.

How would you like to be the one who delivers flowers to hospitals or offices, or the messenger chosen to deliver million dollar checks from a sweepstakes? Work with God. He has a miracle reserved for every lost, searching person. All we have to be is the delivery boy. What a great job! That's our job in the Kingdom! "Flowers from God for you! Here's your inheritance!" Do these four things and you will bear much fruit. A life of ministry will begin to unfold within you.

Even Jezebel Gets a Period of Time in Which to Repent

# 10

# Process and Crisis
# in the Christian Walk

*I*t is important to understand that the spiritual life has both process and crisis in it. In other words, some things happen spiritually in a gradual, sometimes imperceptible way; other things happen all at once in an amazing "breakthrough" moment. When a person comes out of their spiritual blindness and bondage to sin and Satan, their deliverance will have both process and crisis points.

When I was a young soul-winner, I was so afraid of being accountable and so conscious of Hell that I tried to move people to accept the Lord the first time we talked about spiritual things. A scripture in Revelation helped me and made me a more effective witness overall. Here it is:

> *"Nevertheless I have this against you: You tolerate that woman Jezebel, who calls herself a prophetess. By her teaching she misleads my servants into sexual immorality and the eating of food sacrificed to idols. I have given her time to repent of her immorality, but she is unwilling.* (Revelation 2:20–21 NIV, underlining is mine).

A little background may be helpful. The church in Thyatira is being judged by the Lord Jesus. They have allowed a sensual person in their fellowship to teach that immorality is of no importance to God (because the body is just our material part and will die anyway). Through this, some of the servants of God in that church have been weakened in their walk and are now engaged in regular sexual experimentation and immorality. Others are being encouraged to return to the idolatry they have just escaped from. The Lord is chastising the church for being so passive in the face of evil. It is hard to imagine a person doing something more evil than Jezebel in a church.

## A Space to Repent

Verse twenty-one is the part I want to draw your attention to: *"I have given her time to repent of her immorality."* I have to make a confession here. When I see a movie where there is a really, really evil person and it comes to a climax where the gentle, good-hearted person has the gun for once, and has a split-second advantage, something in me yells, "Shoot him now while you have the chance, before he trips you and kills you!" Often the good guy (or girl) is a hesitant enforcer and prolongs the audience's agony while they fumble around with the decision. The end of the thriller has to be when the bad guy gets what is coming to him. That's justice from a human point of view.

We cheer when evil people die and mourn the passing of a righteous person cut down, "before his time." God's perspective is different. The death of the righteous is a time of heavenly celebration. God has His child securely in his arms and nobody will ever hurt them again. When the wicked die, however, the Father groans. Like the prodigal's father, He longs to be reconciled with the wayward and looks for a way to reach them every day. He lives in eternity and sees the reality of Heaven and Hell at all times. We really have no idea how horrible Hell is. Jehovah knows and is a God of mercy as well as justice:

> *"Say to them, 'As surely as I live, declares the Sovereign Lord, I take no pleasure in the death of the wicked, but rather that they turn from their ways*

*and live. Turn! Turn from your evil ways! Why will you die, O house of Israel?"* (Ezekiel 33:11 NIV)

*". . . He is patient with you, not wanting anyone to perish, but everyone to come to repentance."* (2 Peter 3:9 NIV)

Let's return to our text in Revelation 2:21. What I see there totally amazes me. Jezebel is such a horrible person! She is hurting other people daily. You'd think that God would "nuke" her ASAP. But He doesn't. His heart of love gives even Jezebel a space of time in which to repent. God works on her and tries to soften her to lead her to repentance and away from the gates of Hell.

## They Are Under Divine Protection

Here's the application for you and me. If the Father would give wicked old Jezebel a space to repent, we can assume that He does this with everyone else, too, since He isn't a God who plays favorites. The fact that God has led you into a relationship with a particular lost person means that it is now the period of life when God is working on them. He isn't going to let them get killed today. He is reaching out to them through you. You don't have to unnaturally force things to happen quickly lest anything bad should happen. They need the cure for sin and that cure takes several doses to work.

Everyone is at a different level of relatedness to God. Some people are at a minus ten. They hate God and blame Him for whatever pain they have experienced in life. In their anger, they may even insist that He doesn't exist. Others believe in the existence and goodness of God, but just feel a million miles away from Him. Others, lost at level three, feel the emptiness inside. Perhaps they have met a Christian that they admire. Their hearts are softening and they would welcome a conversation about the direction of their lives.

## Helping Them Get to the Zero Point

Let's say that the zero point is where you accept Christ and move into positive numbers of relatedness with God. My job is to use whatever influence I have to move people one step closer to that point than they already are. They can't just jump from a suspicious and hardened minus ten to the zero point in one movement. It is a process. First, their sin has to lead to some trouble and brokenness. Then they have to meet some positive, sincere believers who soften them up with their unconditional love. They need some kind of experience where God reveals Himself through an answered prayer, or in dreams, or other means of revelation. Then they have to get some of the word of God inside to begin working in them. They have to count the cost. They must decide to die to their old life and let God take over. Then, they can finally respond to God's open arms, bow the knee and embrace Jesus as Lord and Savior.

## This is Teamwork

There is an unseen team at work in the salvation of every lost person. The Holy Spirit is the main force. He brings them to conviction and causes the hundreds of little co-incidences needed for their salvation experience to happen. He superintends the entire process. He uses books, bumper stickers, movies, and experiences to speak to their blinded minds. He empowers them to comprehend the things of God. He draws their hearts and prepares them for numerous meetings with children of God, who will feed them with spiritual food through conversations and resources they share with them when they have opportunity. The Holy Spirit drafts numerous human ambassadors and places them in precise points along that person's life path.

Our job is to give a faithful witness to everyone we encounter at a level they can receive. You can rest assured that you aren't the only one God has working on their lives. While you are building a redemptive relationship, the Holy Spirit is doing a private work in their hearts as well.

Sometimes a person is closed to you personally. This is often true of family members. (Even Jesus noted how difficult it is to reach our own blood kin at times.) In cases like this, "back off" and cover them in prayer. Pray especially for God to send another messenger they'll listen to. If there has been a painful history between you, try your best to repair the damage, even if you don't think it was your fault. Love covers a multitude of sins, so pour out sincere love everywhere you can. Most importantly, pray, pray, pray for the lost!

## Spiritual Midwives

In the new birth process, we are more like midwives than mothers. We can travail over the lost, but we cannot make them become born again. "Pushing it" only leads to spiritual abortions. The new birth is a work of God. We can cheer, pray, cry and hold the hand, but only God brings dead people to life. God opens spiritually blind eyes and causes the deaf to hear His voice. Sometimes the midwife encounters a patient who is still weeks from delivery. Other times the baby is "almost" ready. Every now and then, a lady walks into the hospital; the baby has already crowned and it's, "Battle stations! Push! It's time to act now!" On those exciting days, she eases the baby through the birth canal and welcomes him or her into the new world. She pampers them and makes sure they get proper nourishment, protection and care. Soul winning is like that. Different people need different kinds of spiritual care, depending upon where they are in the process of finding God through Christ.

We could also use a legal metaphor. In essence, the lost person has to have a confrontation with God. When you are guilty you dread your day in court. Lost people need to be instructed and encouraged in their decision to face God with their lives. We walk beside them in the process and allow them to know from our experience that confessing their guilt is the way to a fresh start. Going to church or to a Bible study is great, but the fact remains that they have an appointment with God Himself. They have to account for their lives and accept the fact of their guilt. They have to confess their personal wrongs and make restitution where possible, even if it embarrasses them or costs them something. They have to enter a lifestyle of obedient servanthood as disciples of Christ. That's the deal. I can't change it or make it softer. It's their choice and theirs alone. Many will gladly humble themselves and do whatever they have to in order to leave bondage to Satan. Some, like Jezebel, will not. That's not our fault.

### Invest in Their Salvation

Leading people to Christ takes time. "But I don't have any more time!" Sure you do. We all have the same 24 hours each day. It's just a matter of priorities. In eternity, will you be proud of your golf handicap if it meant that you shut out one hundred people God sent into your life? Will you tell God on that day that you didn't have time to build a relationship with even one new lost person each year?

The greatest gift you can give a person, and the only gift that really matters to a lost person, is the gift of attention. When God leads you to someone who is lost and yet, still opens the door to your friendship, you have to take it as an order from God to pursue friendship with them. Go fishing, shopping, travel with them, or carpool even if you don't like it. Schedule one night every other week to do something social with a winnable, lost person. Tithe your time as well as your money. Give the Lord a fixed amount of time each week for investing in the lives of others.

People just sort of "catch" a hunger for God from those who have it already. There is an unseen spiritual influence that flows between the saved and the lost when they open their hearts to each other about the ordinary issues and longings of life. In time, the soil will be softened and the word of God will become planted deep within the heart of the lost. God's word never fails. You are the only Bible most people ever read. They can't read you if you stay inside your house with the door shut.

## One Day They Will Be Ready

We have six children. The day of birth is always the most exciting day of the pregnancy. All the focus shifts from the pregnant mother to the new child. It is a dramatic time. There is pain. We shed tears. At least one of us cries, usually the baby himself. One day, after all the investment of love, prayers and sharing what the Lord Jesus has done for you, the lost person will be sufficiently convicted and convinced. They will open their hearts and want to receive the Lord. When you hear stories of people who witnessed to someone on an airplane and they burst into tears and accepted Christ on the spot, you need to understand that the Christian was simply in the right seat on the right day. Their witnessing that day isn't the whole story. Others have made a contribution through the months and years that God has been preparing the person for salvation.

The point remains, however, that when the time is right someone has to help deliver the baby. It's not as hard as you might imagine. The midwife feels no pain. God brings the new life to the opening of the womb, but someone has to catch the baby and help it enter the world. It is an honor and a privilege to be the one.

## It Takes More than Kindness

Many Christians have tried to say helpful things to the lost that they know. They pray secretly for them. They wish their lost friends would be saved, but they never can bring themselves to the point of asking the person, "Are you ready to turn your life over to God?"

At a friend's birthday party I made friends with an "unruly" lost person. He owned a liquor store and a gun shop (what a mix!). His jokes were generally "over the line" in terms of decency. He stretched me a bit, but I liked him a lot. I developed a burden for him, prayed for him and hoped to be able to say something to him from the Lord. He seemed like the last person who would ever have a spiritual appetite.

A few months later I ran into him again at a cookout. At the table, the subject of God suddenly came up. Everyone was shocked when he said something tender about the Lord. Someone asked, "What's happening with you?" He said that after one of his extended relatives was put in prison for a horribly savage murder, his family felt a tremendous sense of shame. They felt that they were social outcasts nobody wanted to have around.

Here's where boldness comes in. A country pastor heard about the crime and started visiting the prisoner. During a family visit day, he asked the family if they would like him to come to their home once a week to study the Bible with them as a group. They were delighted! The darkness of their present trial made the unconditional love of God even more dramatic. This pastor's boldness to act in an opportune moment fueled the spiritual hunger of this family at a time when they were distraught and confused. The young man I was praying for seldom misses a week of the study.

## The Law of Asking

This story illustrates the law of asking. Jesus said, "Ask and you shall receive." I have learned in recent years how powerful this law is. The number one characteristic of a person who can actually lead others across the threshold from death to life is the willingness to ask if they are ready. Many people will hesitate at the decision point or will not even know what they need to do unless someone asks them, "Would you like to surrender your life to God and ask Jesus to take over *right now*?" You can't rush the processes in the spiritual journey, but you also can't avoid the crisis (decision) moments when action is required. On one of our births, the doctor wasn't there and the nurse, scared of his wrath, wanted Sherry to cross her legs and keep the baby in! That was bad healthcare. When you sense that a person is ready, be a good caregiver: *ask them* if they want to pray. Don't walk away and call a pastor. Don't try to avoid the responsibility. Ask them. Then pray with them.

As I write this book I am leading our church in a building program to give us our first true home base. I need at least $200,000 to build the building. I was praying and thinking about how to raise the funds, since I knew our local pledges were only half that amount. Then I thought of a very successful businessman that I know. We have been friends for years and I have always tried to be a blessing to him. A thought entered my mind, "Ask him to help with a gift of a million pesos ($20,000)." I have never asked him or anyone else for money directly. After thinking it over for a week, I asked him to meet me for lunch, but told him about the building need so he wouldn't feel ambushed at the dinner table. We talked about many things that day. I was trying to work up the courage to ask, when, with exaggerated gestures, he finally prodded me, "Now *what* do you *want* me to *do* for you?" (He's a very successful businessman, remember?) He was reminding me that you never get what you want until you ask. He said yes. Furthermore, he said that he had in his heart to give a million since he heard about our need.

When a receptive person opens their heart and gets close to the point of surrender, all they need is for someone to ask them. It doesn't matter what they pray. You can lead them or tell them to pray out loud on their own. You can "call God up" for them in prayer and then put them on the line, "Lord, this is the day you have been longing for! Jeremy is now ready to come before you and become reconciled to you. Please listen to his heart's sincere prayer right now. . . ." There is no such thing in the Bible as the "sinner's prayer." Jesus never led anyone in any formula of salvation. Nor did any of the apostles. God judges the heart. Lost people have to confess their guilt, repent of their wrongs with practical "bridge-burning" actions and begin to walk in obedience before God as His servants. Lost people must believe that Jesus has paid the price for their sins and then act on the gospel with their life. That is biblical faith (read James). That's how you get right with God.

Having a fruitful soul-winning life is not complicated. We just have to sacrifice our comfort zone to the Lord and look for normal ways of building community with lost people. As the Lord opens doors, simply tell what the Lord has done for you and assure them that God has a plan for their life. When they eventually open up and bring their messy life into the open, just ask them if they would like to surrender their broken pieces to the Lord. No formula. No right or wrong ways. Just be yourself and represent the God who is seeking fellowship with this precious lost child.

> *"Since, then, we know what it is to fear the Lord, we try to persuade men. . . . Christ's love compels us . . .*

*All this is from God, who reconciled us to himself through Christ and gave us the ministry of reconciliation. . . . We are therefore Christ's ambassadors, as though God were making his appeal through us. We implore you on Christ's behalf: Be reconciled to God. God made him who had no sin to be sin for us, so that in him we might become the righteousness of God.* (2 Co. 5:11, 14, 20–21 NIV)

**Simply Eating Food With Lost People
is a Powerful Way to Evangelize.**

# 11

# Your Most Powerful Piece of Furniture

You may not have even noticed it, but God has quietly placed an awesome piece of soul winning equipment right in your home. It is cleverly disguised as a piece of common furniture, yet it has unrivaled potential as an outreach tool. It's your kitchen table. No place in your house is more potent with spiritual power to win the lost. The Bible never explains why, but table fellowship—simply eating food and having an intentionally God-honoring conversation—is as powerful a force for bonding and imparting spiritual strength as a church service. In Luke 6, after Matthew the tax collector accepts the Lord and quits his questionable job, he instinctively invites all his lost friends into his house for a celebration meal. He intentionally includes Jesus too. The Pharisees, seeing the celebration and hearing the noise of lighthearted conversation, complain that Jesus is fraternizing with the devil's people, damaging his reputation. Jesus says, "Nonsense! We're evangelizing!" "It is not the healthy who need a doctor, but the sick. I have not come to call the righteous, but the sinners, to repentance." (Luke 5:31–32 NIV)

## Redemptive Relationships

They'll never care how much you know till they know how much you care. That is especially true in trying to win a lost person to salvation. Before you can ever speak of spiritual things, you have to speak of natural things and demonstrate your sincere concern for them. It's as easy as going next door and inviting your neighbor or someone at work to come to your house for sandwiches, or leftovers, or a cookout or a bowl of soup made from your mother's recipe. Talk about anything. Ask them for the story of their life. Ask about their kids. Show interest in their lives. Tell them about yourself, too. You aren't perfect and neither are they. That makes for a common foundation upon which to build a lifelong friendship. Don't use the formal dining room and nice china. This is an intentionally casual undertaking, designed to remove the barriers between the lost person and a child of God.

When we left the states for our ten-year commitment to Asia, we decided to intentionally move away from the part of the city where the missionaries have tended to congregate (near the school for their kids). We moved 35 miles away (three hours in Manila traffic) into a neighborhood of 30,000 people. It had nice roads and parks, but no church of any kind. South Manila has 2.5 million people and hardly any churches that could reach out to business people (the group we felt called to because of the tremendous potential they have to change things in the nation).

Being new to the country, we had no friendship circle. We knew that we needed friends and so did our children. We also knew that once we got a circle established, it would more or less limit us because we would reach the "friendship saturation" point (how many friendships can you really maintain at one time?). So we moved south and began to build a new friendship circle within our neighborhood. Focusing on them meant that we could more easily spend quality time with them. We intentionally chose to make friends with lost people who seemed open and attracted to us.

## Our First Harvest in Asia

At the community pool on a mercilessly hot summer day, Sherry and I struck up a conversation with a little girl who was swimming nearby. She told us sadly that her parents fought all the time and were going to divorce. In a few seconds her dad swam over and introduced himself. He was a dive instructor. ("Oh boy!" we thought, "Scuba evangelism again!"). Within minutes he was sheepishly sharing the same information his daughter had already given me.

The next day we went to his house to drop off a tape I had made about marital bonding. His wife met us in the driveway as we drove up. Her face showed results of a lifetime pain. She was young and could have been attractive, but she had hurt written all over her. Hard and drawn, she stood square in front of us, glaring at us in suspicion and demanding, "What do you want with my husband?" I replied that we had a tape for him. She read the title on the tape and sighed, "I hope this helps. Something has to help us." Then she dropped her head and began to tear up. Sherry acted with boldness at this sudden vulnerability. "Can we pray with you right now?" Carrie was ready years ago. She was just waiting helplessly for someone to ask. We prayed and cried and felt the Holy Spirit moving among us. God moved into her life and began her new birth process right there on the sidewalk in the glorious daylight.

Their marriage had been founded on drugs and alcohol. Her husband didn't embrace the new change, but she did! We had never seen such determination from anyone. She had now tasted the unconditional love of God. This was life and she knew it! Carrie burned her bridges behind her one by one. She was the first person we led to the Lord in Asia. After fifteen years, she and her daughter are still steadfast in their devotion to the Lord. She is a vibrant witness to all who will listen. Many others have followed in the subsequent months and years, all along the same pattern: sincere friendship first, that led, eventually, to sharing the deep issues of our hearts over food in our homes, culminating in our being able to present the gospel on just the right day to an open heart.

## How to Build a Church on Table Fellowship

Our church in Manila grew from thirteen to one hundred in the first year. We had no church building, no office, no sign and no printed literature of any kind. What was our secret? Eating food with lost people. Informally, different members of the "church of 13" would invite their friends to their homes for dinner parties. Most of these believers were extremely young in their faith. They couldn't yet find Matthew in the Bible, and couldn't explain salvation. Kathy Mueller was one example. She was an agnostic from France who had come to the end of herself, hating her miserable, cold life. In a moment, Jesus revealed himself to her at a beach retreat that some of our ladies had invited her to, and she sobbed for hours. She didn't know exactly what had happened, except that it was Jesus, and that she was forgiven, and had received a new heart. She wanted her friends to have the same experience.

Kathy would invite exactly 32 people to every dinner and seat them at four tables of eight. She selected one Christian couple to place at each table and tried to match them to six lost people with similar human interests. She would seat them and serve the food. With soft background music playing, she circulated among the tables, playing waitress, filling drink glasses and praying. During the night it was always amazing to watch the power of God enter the room. One table would get silent and I would notice that the Christian at the table had found an opportunity to tell their testimony of what Jesus had done for them. They weren't pushy or putting any other religion down. They were telling their personal, first-hand story. Without fail, everyone at the table listened in amazement. And we really could tell some amazing stories. One of us was formerly a Moslem, raised in Tehran. He had hated Christians. Then God revealed Himself to Mansour and began to work miracles of forgiveness in his life. I had a drug abuse story. Another man had been successful in life, but had nearly destroyed his marriage by infidelity (a national pastime here) until Jesus saved him and his entire household. Sherry had always been "good," but she also had her own story of needing a savior and finding one in Christ.

When those of us at one table saw the other tables becoming anointed we would silently pray for them. Eventually, it would happen at our table too. We won a hundred of our friends in about a year. It cost all of us money for food and took up most of our weekends that year, but it was the richest and most rewarding year of our life in ministry (since then, we have spent most of our time caring for that original harvest and coaching them as they reach out and embrace thousands of others)

## Build Bridges Not Walls

Somebody in the body of Christ has to take the responsibility to establish redemptive relationships with the lost. Relationships are the most powerful tools by which the Holy Spirit transfers the power of God from one life to another. Those who want to build bridges avoid religious clichés and arguing over any topic of religion. In the Philippines, the hot buttons are the worship of idols and the veneration of Mary. These are two extremely important doctrinal issues, but they are not things I can easily discuss with a spiritually blind person. Remember 2 Corinthians 4:4, which said that the devil has blinded the eyes of unbelievers so that they cannot see the truth about Jesus Christ and understand the things of God? Lost people are blind. Period. They misunderstand even that which they think they know about God. We have to avoid needless, premature arguments and look for common ground with the lost. We must build friendships strong enough to take the strain of the spiritual war that will soon take place over their souls.

In general, I do not approach issues that take a spiritually mature mind to comprehend. After a person has received Christ, they will have His Spirit inside of them to guide and teach them (John 14 & 16). At that time they can understand about the evils of idolatry. We can burn their idols together. They will learn the proper place of respect for Mary. They will eventually stop smoking, abusing alcohol and fornicating. That's a given after the Holy Spirit begins bear fruit in their lives (Gal. 5:22). For now I will just build bridges with them and wait for God to do His work.

## We Had to Buy an Ash Tray

In the first year of our friendship-evangelism experience in Manila, we came to a decision point. We had rented a bright white house no one had ever lived in before. Sherry bought two sofas with crisp yellow floral upholstery. She had matching curtains made. Her house was an expression of her personality, and it was really beginning to look great. It would have stayed that way too, except for "those lost people." In Asia, thanks to aggressive advertising by tobacco firms, it seems that most lost people smoke. Imported cigarettes cost only thirty-five cents a pack here, and there are no practical restrictions on age, so most teens take up the habit to impress their peers, then spend the rest of their lives saddled with it. When we invited people into our house, and especially if we were having a serious conversation, they would instinctively reach for their pack and light up. (It isn't considered rude here so they didn't think to ask first).

About halfway through their cigarette, it would become embarrassing for all of us. We had no ashtrays. They would cup their hand apologetically under the drooping ash, the conversation would stop, and they would nervously look for a solution. We could see in their eyes that they were trying to process this strange situation. I imagine it was something like this, "No ashtray? What kind of house has no ashtray? There's something strange about this. Oh, so that's what Christians are about! No smoking!"

To be honest, we didn't want them smoking in our house. We thought they would get the message if there were no ashtrays. We were sacrificing time and energy to get to know them, but there had to be a line drawn somewhere to say, "We will go this far into your world, but no more." Smoking was the line. Smoke made the curtains stink. People burned the new upholstery by carelessly waving their firebrands around. Our kids might be tempted to imitate the grown ups. Then there's the damage of second-hand smoke.

For a few weeks we felt justified, then the Holy Spirit reminded us that lost people are lost. That's why they smoke. They had to overcome a hundred prejudices and the hindrances of Satan to even enter our house in the first place. Was this really such a big deal that we had to risk embarrassing them and possibly losing the opportunity to witness, just to save ourselves the unpleasant experience of having to endure a few minutes of their smoking? Who gave you these curtains anyway? Whose house is this? Whose temple is your body? (We had to admit that protection from brief exposures to second-hand smoke during times of evangelism probably qualifies for the "any deadly thing" protection promise of Mark 16).

Every husband knows that he is really living in his wife's house. I knew it was up to Sherry to decide and that she had to do it from her heart. One day she came back from the grocery store with an ashtray. I was proud of my wife.

The funny thing was that once we had made the decision and purchased the ashtray, hardly anyone ever smoked again in our house.

## The Comfort Zone and the Gates of Hell

Missions leaders estimate that 100,000 new people enter Hell each day. Broken down it means that in every 60 minute period over 4,000 people around the world die without Christ and the hope of Heaven. The deeper tragedy here is *that there are less than ten lost people for every professing believer*. In my opinion, the greatest reason the lost will die lost, is a simple place called the "comfort zone." Instinctively, every adult builds a comfortable life for himself and settles into it. We resist anything that forces us out of our comfortable circle. We feel strange in the homes of others. We also don't like others to come into our homes because then we have to clean it extra well and impress them. We like to watch TV or get on the computer two or three hours every night. We don't like to spend extra money. So the lost go to Hell as we watch Monday night football. Beloved, we are made for higher things. Eternity is coming for all of us sooner than we think.

# 12

# Speaking Prophetically

1 Corinthians 14 tells us that the most important spiritual gift, in terms of the evangelistic mission of the church, is the gift of prophecy:

> *". . . Eagerly desire spiritual gifts, especially the gift of prophecy."* (1 Co. 14:1b NIV)

Are you eagerly desiring spiritual gifts, *especially prophecy*, as instructed by the scriptures?

As a child I was always thrilled (and terrified) with horses. They are so huge and deadly, but to sit on the back of a horse and gallop at full speed is one of the most exciting things a person can ever do in life. When I turned forty I decided that I would revisit my lifelong fear/fascination and learn to do more than hang on to the saddle and yell, "Ha! Giddy up!" So, I found a qualified teacher and have worked diligently every week to become a great horseman. It is hot, hard, and at times, frightening work, but I *eagerly desire* to do it. Again, are you eagerly desiring to be used by God in the gift of prophecy?

## What is it?

Most people think of prophets as men with long beards who stand alone on a mountain and cry out prophecies to their nation and their king. In the Old Testament, that's not too far from the truth, but everything in God's plan changed when Jesus came. The New Testament reveals that, because of Calvary, the Holy Spirit is now poured out upon all of God's people. We all become temples of the Holy Spirit. The gifts are liberally distributed among us and the anointing of the Spirit is poured out like a ceaseless rain upon the entire body of Christ. In short, New Testament prophets are ordinary people who work 9 to 5 jobs, wash dishes and raise kids. New Testament believers can *all* prophesy in church (1 Co. 14:31) or, more importantly, for evangelistic purposes, over a cup of coffee with a friend, or at school.

Without going into a detailed study of the function of the gift of prophecy, let me summarize that prophecy is essentially, "delivering a message from God to someone He wants to talk to." Most of the time, prophecy is directed to those who are seeking to hear from God (whether they are aware of it or not). The purpose of the prophecy is for the recipient's faith to be ignited so that they will obey the Lord and so that their relationship with God becomes deeper. The prophet's task is to faithfully deliver God's message and to edify (build up, strengthen) the recipient in the process.

### Process and Crisis

There is process and crisis in most things connected to the spiritual pathway, and it is true of prophecy also. There is a moment of decision (that's what the word "crisis" means) when a disciple realizes that God wants to use them to be His spokesperson. At that place, we must bow and accept the prophet's role by faith, trusting that God will supply the words and the anointing to deliver them well. After this *crisis* of decision, there follows the ongoing *process* of learning how to better execute this kind of ministry. Isaiah makes a good case study.

Isaiah is called to be a prophet in the dramatic sixth chapter of his book. He is a prince, living in the royal city. His mentor, King Uzziah, has died. Isaiah goes into the temple to pray, groaning, no doubt, about the leadership vacuum in the land. There aren't enough men of God! The people are slipping deeper into immorality and godlessness by the day. In an instant, Isaiah receives a revelation of the Lord Jehovah in all His majestic splendor. He sees that Jehovah is the true King of Israel and that, unlike Uzziah, He will never die!

Suddenly surrounded by the presence of the perfect God, Isaiah feels the weight of his own sinfulness and imperfections. He is a sinner, full of inconsistencies and shortcomings. Becoming aware of his own sinfulness, he feels unworthy to be near God. He even fears that God's holiness might suddenly destroy him because of his sin. "I am a man of unclean lips!" he cries out in confession. An angel burns his lips to purge them (and maybe to teach him to talk less and listen more, especially for now).

### God's Only Problem

On his face before God, Isaiah overhears God talking about His only problem.

> *"Whom shall I send? And who will go for us?"*
> God laments.

This is a persistent problem. God has always had it, and sadly, probably always will unless the church, in our day, undergoes a radical change. God has a shortage of spokesmen (prophets). This was true in Isaiah's day, and it was still true in Christ's time. Jesus told the twelve, "Pray! The harvest is great, but the laborers are few!" The devil works around the clock. He knows that his time is limited, and he wants to take as many people to Hell with him as possible. God's heart is simultaneously reaching out to the lost and wayward every moment! He is willing to forgive them. Jesus has paid the price already and everyone can go free! Nobody has to go to Hell! If they only knew—if only someone would speak to them for God!

Isaiah's heart is exploding. The Father has so graciously taken away his sin. Understanding that the Almighty is now having trouble finding someone to be His helper moves Isaiah past his fears. He can't control his response. He shouts out, "Here am I. Send me!" Can you imagine, for a moment, how the Father felt that day? Think about what this voluntary action did to the burdened heart of God! Isaiah ministered to the Lord's need for someone to send, and consequently, enters the ranks of those called prophets.

How about you? Can you hear the Father's voice? Can you feel His great heart beating for His lost children who will never know Him? The first time many of the lost will ever hear His voice will be to hear, "Depart from me into outer darkness." How do you think that makes Him feel? You could volunteer if you wanted to. You could leave the self-centered life we all start with and enter the ranks of the prophets and ambassadors who work the harvest field of humanity every day. You could be an Isaiah. It all starts with getting near enough to God to feel His pain over the lost. Once you really feel it, only a cold, heartless person could keep from standing and shouting like Isaiah, "Here am I. Send me!"

## How Do I Prophesy?

Here's where the process part comes in. Read Isaiah 50:4. It describes the process Isaiah went through over the next 40 years as he learned, by daily practice, how to walk in the gift of prophecy.

> "The Sovereign LORD has given me an instructed tongue, to know the word that sustains the weary.

*He wakens me morning by morning, wakens my ear
to listen like one being taught."* (Isaiah 50:4 NIV)

Remember Isaiah's "besetting sin?" In chapter six he con-
fesses that he doesn't steward his speech ability properly.
He uses his mouth to complain, curse and speak ill of
others. He is negative and hurtful in his speech. He tears
others down. He does not honor God with his lips. Decades later, Isaiah is now a seasoned man of God. Note the
change in him and how it was accomplished. God has
trained his tongue.

Back to my horses. A horse is a huge animal. He may weigh
over a ton. He can dominate any man and easily injure or
kill him. The only good use for a horse would be to provide meat, except for this one characteristic: if you can get
a horse to take a small metal bit into his mouth you can
control his movements and actions. The control of his
mouth alone causes the horse to become a useful partner
in the service of mankind. No other animal has been as in-
strumental in the march of man's progress.

It's the same with humans in the service of God. Being useful to God begins with gaining control of the mouth. God
has to be the Lord and Master of our tongues. He has to
train us with commands like, "Silence!" "Speak gently,"
and "Sing!" We have to learn how to return a soft word for
a harsh one and to stop speaking out our frustrations with
people, and quit giving vent to our bigotry. Our tongue
has to go to obedience school.

## God Worked on Me

As a young pastor, I noticed that in times of tension with
others I always seemed to be on the losing end. Whatever
I said, even if I thought I had good intentions, always
seemed to make things worse. Sometimes I wrote people

letters to clarify things. That never worked well either. Living in Jamaica, I angered the sour-faced postmistress so that she refused to ever give me my mail again. I had to send a Bible school student or a boy to the desk to get it. This lasted over two years. I finally realized that the problem must be in me, but I couldn't understand what it was. "Lord, change me!" I sighed. He did.

First, we worked on my sense of humor. I was raised in a quick-witted family. We have a wisecracking ability that kept us in stitches whenever we were in a car together or having a family meal. It wasn't malicious, but tended to be sarcastic. Many times I would poke fun at the failures of others. As kids, we mocked the "strange" people in our lively church. I had never questioned this habit, because it was just part of being me.

The Lord spoke to me one day, "You are scornful of others." I thought about what that word meant. To be scornful is to feel superior. A scornful person marks well the faults of others and mocks them for having these weaknesses. I had to admit that the Lord was right on target. I often interrupted others when they were speaking, finishing the sentence for them if they got stuck for words. If I walked into a place, I instinctively started fixing things. "Why didn't anyone think of parking spaces when they built this place?" I would ask myself, often out loud. I noticed that I heard the squeaky ending note rather than the otherwise perfect performance of a song. If that was in my heart, it had to be coming out in my gestures, tone of voice and timing.

Rev. Sam Vassal came to preach for me one Sunday. I'll never forget his words: "Humble people receive from God, that which they do not deserve." Sister Reid had always told me, "Humility is the path to greatness." I had tried to be humble and I expected to make greater progress now that I had named my "demon" and could work on eliminating that habit from my life. (Early Christian spiritual advisors considered it essential that a growing disciple be able to name the things in his life that were holding him back. They felt that by naming and renouncing it out loud they could better gain control over these things than by privately straining to stop the habits).

That year, for Christmas, I gave Jesus the gift of getting scorn out of my heart and life. It took the entire year, but I gradually got the beast under control and honestly began to enjoy people, considering their weaknesses less than my own. From time to time this old monster attempts to stir again, usually when I am tired spiritually and physically. At those times, I again have to put my mind and tongue under "heavy manners" (that's what Jamaicans call it when you have to tighten up the controls on an unruly child, punishing every little wrong for a time, until he bows his will and submits to his parent's rule). Discipline breaks the power of the flesh.

As I went to war with my poor attitude, I started getting along with everyone. I even became a peacemaker, able to quickly settle things in a "win-win" way even with mean-tempered people. I now love people genuinely from my heart. This is the first step toward becoming a true prophet.

## The Spirit of a True Prophet

Some people claim to be prophetic when all they are is self-righteous. They love to be the teacher and desire to dominate the lives of others "in the name of the Lord." They love the power associated with the offices of ministry and the gift of prophecy. Great pain is caused as they rebuke and "beat the sheep" with their admonitions. These are not prophets. They are spiritual infants (1 Co. 14:20), still in their diapers. The spirit of a true prophet is revealed in the way he feels about the people he is speaking to:

> *"But everyone who prophesies speaks to men for their strengthening, encouragement, and comfort."*
> (1 Co. 14:3 NIV)

Only when we love the people God has created can the Father use us to speak to them for their "strengthening, encouragement and comfort."

## No Irritating God Talk

When we first start trying to speak to the lost for God we usually go about it in the wrong way. We slide "spiritual" words into otherwise normal conversations in a forced way. We may talk about the wonderful revival we are having "down at the church." We might chide them when they cuss or light up a smoke. Maybe we drop in "I'm praying for you!" as our way of saying goodbye. In reality, Christian bumper stickers and God-talk are mostly just an irritation to the lost. It is an obvious attempt to influence them to be like us and generally conveys the message that we feel superior morally and ethically to them. My advice is to skip it entirely. Jesus said, "Just let your 'Yes' be 'Yes.'" I think that means that we should use normal plain language and keep our sentences short enough to control the meanings.

Instead of trivializing the power of the gospel with "God-talk" just wait until you can prophesy to them. What do I mean? I'll give an example. For a holiday Sherry and I took our family to Boracay. In case you don't know, Boracay is one of the last jewels in the Philippines, a small island with white sand and clear, azure water. It is a "secret" usually known only to German eco-tourists who come for the sunshine and the atmosphere. Many have stayed for years, opening up dozens of small gourmet restaurants housed in bamboo huts with sand floors. Nothing can be built taller than a coconut tree and music surrounds you no matter where you go. There is no road, just a sand path that links these mom and pop establishments into an unbroken two-mile chain of dive shops, restaurants and $20-a-night bungalows.

Getting there is half of the adventure: big plane to bus, to motorcycle, to raft, to small boat, and finally, to the island. The journey begins at the Manila domestic airport. You can tell who is going to Boracay. Some are backpackers from Israel. Some are local people already decked out in flowery shirts and straw hats. Others are hedonistic guys from Europe who have heard of the place and the cheap beer. They usually pay for a package deal that includes a prostitute as your escort for the entire time. Some take two girls. As I surveyed the airport that day, my eyes fastened on a young man standing alone by the air-conditioner in the corner. He had no girls. No friends either. He was well kept. I thought how unusual he seemed in this crowd. He came and sat beside me later on the small boat that ferries you across the shark-infested channel to the island. We struck up a conversation.

"So, Mark, what brings you to Boracay?"

"I came for the fishing," he replied.

(Now Boracay has many things, but nobody would ever dream of coming there for deep sea fishing. Even the dive shops have to put food in the water near their dive sites, just to try to attract some fish so everyone will have something besides sand to look at. I knew this must be the Lord.)

"Where are you staying?" I asked.

"I have no idea." he replied, "It was crazy of me. I just bought a ticket, got on a plane in Hong Kong where I live, and here I am. No plan at all."

"Oh," I said, "Then you should stay at our little hotel. I'll get a good price for you."

He was happy for the help and checked in along with us. When we went to dinner that night we saw him sitting alone on his porch and invited him to eat with us. We walked to a bamboo, beachfront restaurant that served Hungarian food. As our food arrived, I asked if I could pray for the meal and just said a simple prayer of thanks for the safe journey, the daily bread, and our new friend. We had no sooner said our "Amen" than Mark blurted out, "What religion are you?" I tried to answer in as delicate a way as possible. I didn't want him to pigeonhole us into some mental category of his and cut us off from being able to speak to him about Christ. He didn't let me finish my sentence.

"I hate my life!" he said with great emotion to the two strangers seated across the table from him. Then, he poured out his story of being raised in an incredibly wealthy family and all the dysfunction that wealth had brought with it. He told of being trapped in a meaningless existence. We just listened for a long time, then I prophesied to him. It went something like this:

> "Mark, it is no accident that we are all here at this table. When I saw you in the airport something inside of me said that you were a special person. I knew it was from God when you came and sat next to me. There is no fishing here. I think God just made you believe it so we could meet. God knows that you are empty and searching. He is reaching out to you today. He has a wonderful plan to give you a mean-

*ingful life, and He arranged for us to meet so we can explain to you how to find it."* Then we explained the gospel to him at a level he could understand and told him what Jesus had done in our lives.

I felt the Holy Spirit's powerful anointing upon me that starry night as I delivered what I felt in my heart was God's personalized message to this searching young man. You don't have to say, "Thus saith the Lord!" to prophesy, especially to the lost (it would probably scare them to death!). Just deliver God's message to them in a passionate, but conversational way.

To summarize, in evangelizing relationships let's skip all the God-chatter and clichés and, instead, wait for the appointed day. When that day comes, the person you have been praying for and building a redemptive relationship with will open up the door to you. On that day, as you see the drawbridge to their heart lowered in front of you, seize the opportunity, lock eyes with them and represent God to them in a personal and powerful way.

> *"We are therefore Christ's ambassadors, as though God were making his appeal through us. We implore you on Christ's behalf: Be reconciled to God."* (2 Co. 5:20 NIV)

Be a prophet! Allow God to speak powerfully to lost people through your trained heart and lips!

# 13

# Just Stand at the Door

*I* read a poem years ago that I have since lost and can't locate anywhere. I never knew who wrote it, so if you are out there and get your hands on a copy of this book, hats off to you! I wish I could credit you by name. The poem was entitled, "I Stand at the Door." The vision of that poem is a fitting way to end this short book. I'll try to recreate it for you in prose.

*Years ago I entered into the wonderful family of God and was admitted into the glorious fellowship they enjoy. The doors to the church were opened wide to me and I have been feasting and enjoying the loving company of God's family ever since. Every day is a celebration of sharing, loving and laughing. Eating together, we swap stories, bear each other's burdens and grow daily in the grace and knowledge of our Lord and His word. Most of us go so deep inside God's house that we completely forget that there are many people shivering in the cold outside, having never found this wonderful warm haven. So, I stand at the door.*

*I watch the dark, danger-filled streets for those who are groping for a door. Persistently, they search, knowing that a door to God and to peace has to exist. There must be a door! They try many doors, frantically. Each one leads to more pain and disappointment. Some just give up, sit in the streets and die. Others push ahead, stumbling, bruised and bleeding, crying out for help. That's why I stand at the door, inside the house of God, enjoying their fellowship, but not too far inside, lest I lose sight of the streets outside.*

> *There is only one door and I cannot open it for any-
> one else. The door only opens to a man's own touch.
> But the outsiders are bound with spiritual blindness.
> They cannot see the door and without help they will
> never be able to find it. That's why I stand at the
> door. Maybe that's why David said, "I'd rather be a
> doorkeeper in the house of the Lord. . . ."*

You can be a different kind of Christian. Just go stand by
the door every day and take care of the ones God sends
your way. We hope sharing our story with you will help
you get started. Please email us your testimonies of how
God uses you in the harvest. If you will apply the four
simple steps we mentioned, you will be able to stand before the Father at the end of your life and bring Him fruit.
You can bring joy to the heart of God. The gift He desires
is to see His lost children back home.

Receiving your victory stories will be a great encouragement to us. My address is chuck@quinley.com. May God
bless our harvest as we all join hands together and wade
into the ripened harvest fields.

> *"I tell you, open your eyes and look at the fields! They
> are ripe for harvest. Even now the reaper draws his
> wages, even now he harvests the crop for eternal
> life. . . ."*—Jesus (John 4:35–36 NIV)

# Signing the 30 Day Covenant
## (Test-driving Relational Evangelism)

*T*wo of the greatest enemies of fruitful evangelism are guilt and pressure. Just try the simple method we have been describing for the next 30 days. During that enlightening period the Lord will use you to bear fruit and you will enter into that intimate joy that only harvesters ever know. You will be changed and so will the course of your Christian life. It all starts with a simple determination to step out of the comfort zone for one short month. I really do hope that you will sign the commitment below and enter the harvest field, working alongside our Lord.

## *My Covenant*

"My loving Father, knowing that your heart is burdened today about the millions of men, women and children who are lost to you, I commit myself for the next thirty days to practice the four step principles of this book. Every day I will:

1. Pray, "God, send me someone who needs your help today."
2. Tune-in to other people, connecting with them by loving and listening until someone opens up to me about a problem in their personal life.
3. Declare and brag on Jesus to those persons, telling all he has done for me and for so many others.
4. Offer to pray on the spot with those who open their hearts to me and share their needs.

I cannot do this in my own strength, so I am trusting you to provide the courage and supernatural anointing I need for this mission by the power of your Spirit working in me.

In the name of Jesus I will love the lost and interact with them in building redemptive relationships so that they can find You and know the peace I have found in your arms.

Thank you for calling and using me in the harvest field with your Son.

This is my covenant with you.

*Signed:* _____

*Date:* _____

*Witnessed by my pastor or friend:* _____

# Appendix

# Seeker's Bible Study Lessons

*T*en years ago a young man named John Sentz came to me and asked me to disciple him. I love John and sincerely wanted to see him grow into maturity as the man of God I knew he was, but to be honest, when he asked me to "disciple him," I didn't really know where to start. This Christian life is so wonderful and what I knew about the Lord had taken me a lifetime to acquire. That event, however, started me on a course of thinking as a pastor. If I didn't know how to disciple someone, then who did?

The following material is a resource guide for any pastor, church leader or mature Christian, who wants to be a spiritual guide to other people. This is a curriculum intended for a small group or an individual Bible study with those who are seeking to know the truth about God and spiritual things in general. These lessons require very little prior knowledge of the Bible. The goal of the Spiritual Pathway Lessons is to lead the seeker to a full understanding of the gospel and to influence them to commit their lives to Jesus Christ as Lord. My paradigm of disciple making is "obedience-based discipleship." It is also crucial to me as a pastor that I focus the heart of the new disciple upon the person and teachings of Jesus Christ himself. I think it is of utmost importance that every disciple place the words of Jesus in the highest position of authority. My focus throughout these studies is, therefore, largely grounded in the study of the gospels, versus a survey of the entire Bible.

God blessings on you as we reap the harvest together!

CHUCK QUINLEY
MANILA, PHILIPPINES

## Pathways 1: The Truth Will Set You Free

### Approach:

*Q: Did you believe in Santa when you were a child? How did you find out the truth? How did you feel when you discovered he was only make-believe?*

This lesson is about the power of truth to set us free. The problem with truth is that it is often painful to our ego to discover that we are wrong. We often resist the truth if it is different from what we have always believed. Sometimes we resist the truth about ourselves because it is painful to be corrected. We can never walk on God's spiritual pathways until we determine to love truth and welcome it at all times, no matter how it comes to us. All truth is God's truth. All truth is good for us and will help us grow and walk properly. In order to be a disciple of Jesus Christ, we must all be earnest seekers of truth.

*Q: What is the difference between "truth" and "opinion?"*

**Bible Exploration:** The Path of Truth

***Principle 1:*** God wants everyone to know the truth
(Read 1 Tim. 2:4)

***Principle 2:*** We can't find the truth by ourselves because our inner nature has been corrupted by sin. In order to accurately receive truth it must be revealed to us by the God of truth.

*Q: How does the absence of that accurate guidance hinder our spiritual search for truth?*

– *2 Corinthians 4:4* Before we receive a new birth in Christ, our minds are clouded with spiritual blindness. We do not think or understand things properly without God's assistance.

– *2 Timothy 3:7* Despite earnest human searching we will never find the truth by our own power. No "inner search" can find the answers. We have to seek the truth from God himself.

– *2 Timothy 4:4* We tend to accept only those things that match our previous "learning." In seeking to hear things we agree with already, we can end up believing myths and rest on our opinions, etc., as though they were settled truth.

– *2 Corinthians 3:16* When we turn to Jesus for new birth, the blindness is removed and we have the new capacity to receive truth directly from God and to see things as they truly are.

**Principle 3:** In His love, God has given us three reliable guides to lead us to the truth.

**1.** The Bible is God's objective record of truth by which we judge everything in life.
– 2 Timothy 3:14–17.

*Q: How does it benefit humanity to have an objective, changeless book of truth to guide us?*

**2.** Jesus came to us as God's personal messenger in human flesh to reveal the truth to us and to free us from the power of deception that held our minds captive.
– John 8:42–47; 17:8; 18:37

*Q: How would sending a personal human representative safeguard the communication of truth from God to us?*

**3.** God has sent His Holy Spirit into the world to act as an inner guide for those who seek the truth from Him. The Holy Spirit will lead us daily as we search the scriptures to understand what is true and how to live according to the truth.

– *John 14:17 (NIV)* "[The Holy Spirit] is the Spirit of truth. The world cannot accept Him, because it neither sees Him nor knows Him. But you know Him, for He lives with you and will be with you."

– *John 16:13 (NIV)* "But when He, the Spirit of truth, comes, He will guide you into all truth. He will not speak on His own; He will speak only what He hears, and He will tell you what is yet to come."

*Q: Why is it important for God to place an inner guide to truth inside of those who want to follow Him? Are you actively praying to God for the Holy Spirit's guidance in learning new truth?*

**Principle 4:** Every truth we discover will set us free

*John 8:32 (NIV)* "Then you will know the truth, and the truth will set you free." Our new spiritual life begins when we open our hearts and minds to the truth and begin having an honest relationship with God and others.

Q: *Have you ever had the experience of being set free by the discovery of a new truth? How does truth set us free?*

**Principle 5:** We must always act in obedience to every truth we discover.

– *John 3:21* When we live by the truth, everyone will see that God is working in our lives.

– *James 1:22* Those who hear the truth must obey it in their daily actions. We are accountable to live by truth once we know it.

Refusing to listen to and love the truth can lead to our own destruction (Read 2 Thess. 2:10)

Q: *Can you think of an example where a person's refusal to accept the truth led to an even greater suffering? Determine to be a teachable person from this moment on, so that you can learn truths from God, His Word, and others.*

**Life Application:** Searching for Truth in all the Wrong Places

Most of us are, at some level, "seekers of spiritual truth." Someone long ago coined the phrase "the God-shaped Void" to describe the emptiness that seems to be at the center of the human heart as we walk in our lives alone, cut off from meaningful fellowship with our Creator God, and His truth. Much of our human pursuit of happiness is an attempt to fill up this emptiness with things we can manufacture or obtain on our own apart from God. It never quite works because the space inside is reserved for Him and only He can fill it. This void is a beacon to call us home to fellowship with Him. This is the reason we were created. The short Bible book of Ecclesiastes is the story of a man who was, in his lifetime, the worlds wealthiest, most educated and most powerful. Solomon, King of Israel, had an annual income, from conquered nations alone, of 25 tons of gold (over $300 million). He had ongoing sexual relations with nearly 1,000 of the world's most beautiful women and accomplished massive building projects, ruling over his nation for 40 years without any challenge to his power. Yet at the end of it all he cries, "Meaningless! Meaningless! Everything is utterly meaningless!" He writes his book to tell his many children not to follow in his ways. He ends his book telling them that real peace and fulfillment is found only in knowing God and walking in His truth. Open your heart to God and His voice as He guides you to truth.

**Action Steps:**
– This week ask yourself, "What human pursuits am I doing to try and fill the God-shaped void? Am I willing to come to God alone for my contentment?"

– This week begin the habit of reading one chapter of the Bible each day. Try reading Mark, Luke or John. Before reading, always stop and pray that the Holy Spirit will guide you into truth and help you to get the message God is speaking to you.

– This week pray each day saying, "Lord send me someone today who needs your help." Then be on the lookout for the person and pray about what encouraging thing to say or do for them.

**Memory Verse:** *John 8:32 (NIV)* "Then you will know the truth, and the truth will set you free."

## Pathways 2: The Great Exchange

**Goal:** This lesson will help you understand God's loving plan to remove our guilt and sin from us.

### Approach:

Recently, the papers carried the remarkable story of a man who asked his pastor to accompany him as he turned himself in for a murder which he had committed fifteen years prior to accepting Christ, getting married and having a family. The police had no evidence against him and could never have discovered him as the murderer. (He had been drunk and had killed a young lady who startled him as he was robbing the house). He said that he was guilty whether they caught him or not and that he couldn't live with this unconfessed sin any more.

*Q: What would you do in a similar circumstance?*

*Q: Can guilty person ever erase the fact and condition of their guilt?*

### Bible Exploration:

*The Scapegoat and the Sacrifice:* In Leviticus 16 God gave the Jewish people a ritual to teach them about His plan to remove the guilt of their personal sins (Read Lev. 16:6–10). Two spotless sacrifices were chosen to bear the responsibility for the sins of the people, although they were totally innocent themselves.

The first was killed to pay the penalty of their sins. Its life's blood was poured out before God in place of the blood of the guilty. The second goat was led to the wilderness (where the devil lived, according to local superstition).

The priest placed his hands on the goat and declared that the sins and guilt of all the people had been transferred to the goat that would now bear their shame and carry it away from them. That goat was released to "take to the devil" the guilt of the people. The goat was never seen again. (Read Lev. 19:21–22)

By observing this custom yearly the people became aware of the reality of their sins, their need for a savior and the existence of a plan in the mind of God to cleanse them.

**Truth 1:** Jesus came to be the blood sacrifice for our sins once and for all (Heb. 9:12)

– There will never be another sacrifice (Heb. 9:24–28)

– No other sacrifice is acceptable to God (Heb. 10:10)

– Nothing can add to or diminish this holy sacrifice (Heb. 10:14)

**Truth 2:** Jesus came to be the scapegoat, carrying our guilt and shame into the wilderness of death and the grave (2 Cor. 5:21)

### My New Identity in Christ
Anyone who accepts the sacrifice of Christ on their behalf starts life again as a new person with a new identity, free from the guilt of their previous life.

– I am reborn into a new life in Christ. My past is gone. (2 Cor. 5:17)

– I have become a temple in which God's eternal Spirit resides, guides and acts (1 Cor. 3:16)

– I am totally accepted and unconditionally loved by God apart from my own worthiness or performance because I am eternally identified with Christ and covered with his blood. (Gal. 2:20; 1 Th. 1:4)

– I have been equipped with a mix of powerful supernatural abilities uniquely suited to my personality and God's plan to use me. (Ro. 12:4–8)

– My destiny in this life and the next is secure in Christ. (1 Jn. 3:1–2)

– My life has meaning. I am a member of the Royal Family of God laboring under my Father as His Kingdom comes to earth. (1 Pe. 2:9–10)

### Life Application:

### Process and Crisis in the Spiritual Life:

*The Spiritual path offered by Jesus has two important dimensions:* process and crisis. On the one hand there is a gradual process of self-discipline under God's new governance. By this our character and lifestyle are continually being purified and transformed into His image. Like an athlete in training, we stretch our moral fiber and build spiritual muscle daily as we walk in obedience with Christ.

On the other hand, there are these wonderful instant flashes of grace by which we gain many great victories supernaturally. Decision-points are reached in a flash of insight. We receive dramatic release from old resentment, vices, and emotional depression by the power of the Spirit of God at work in us. In both of these ways God continues His work in us and we go "from glory to glory" along the path with Him. Expect both of these dimensions of the Spirits work in you.

### Action Steps:

– Determine to allow Jesus to be the scapegoat for your sins carrying away any shame you feel for your past choices in life. Tell God in prayer whatever you are ashamed of and ask Him to send it away forever. Refuse to ever dwell on it again.

– Wake up every morning this week thanking Jesus for sacrificing himself for you.

**Memory Verse:** *2 Cor. 5:21* "God made him who had no sin to be sin for us, so that in him we become the righteousness of God."

# *Pathways 3: No Other Name?*

## Approach:

*Q: What's the greatest price you have ever had to pay to move ahead in life?*

## Bible Exploration: No Other Name

Because the death of Jesus was the greatest act of love and humility in the history of the universe, God is rightly disgusted at any human effort to disregard the sacrifice of his dear Son. Any effort to establish a worthiness of our own based on our own work rather than accepting the very lifeblood that Jesus sacrificed is considered by God as just another act of rebellion against Him. We cannot, by any means of our own, no matter how sincere, erase the fact of our guilt and make ourselves acceptable before God.

### *The Stumbling Block*

The thing about Jesus that irritates modern thinkers (ever notice how few positive references to Jesus or Christianity there are in movies, etc., even though most of the great hospitals, colleges and mercy organizations in the world were established by Christians?) is his refusal to be considered as "just another" possible door to God. Eastern mysticism, for example, is very much en vogue in Hollywood and the media because you can make up the rules for yourself and answer to no one but your own "inner voice." (Read Jn. 10:7–11; 14:6) Let's study the Bible's teaching about the supremacy of Jesus Christ.

### *The Claims of Jesus*

1. Jesus has earned the highest place in the universe by his being God, by His conquest of Satan, and by his sacrifice for us (Phil. 2:9).

2. He will not accept second place to anything or anyone (Luke 14:26, the distance between loyalty to Christ and loyalty to anyone else must be a gap as wide as love from hate).

3. Jesus is the ultimate and final revelation of God to mankind. He is the only completely reliable human teacher. Everything he says is an accurate word from God to men. Anyone who

has ever taught any other way to God has been either sincerely mistaken or deliberately sent by Satan to confuse people (Matt. 24:35; Jn. 5:24).

4. No one else can be compared to Jesus. Even in the scriptures, his teachings have the highest authority and must be the primary source of any doctrine or ministry practice (Matt. 5:31–42, Jesus has authority to "upgrade" the Old Testament scriptures). All Christian teaching has to conform to his. Alignment to the words of Jesus is the test of all prophecy: 1 John 4:2–3; Revelations 19:10.

5. Anyone clinging to any other hope or offering any other plan is simply deluded and heading for trouble no matter how sincere they might be or how hard they are working to build a righteousness with God apart from Christ (Luke 6:47–49).

6. Jesus is King over all earthly sources of authority (government, parents, employers, etc.) and must be obeyed over them whenever their commands conflict with his (Acts 5:29–31; Rev. 17:14).

7. Jesus is Lord over the spirit world. All demons bow to Him. All God's angels, Mary and all the apostles bow in reverence before Him (Phil. 2:10–11).

8. Jesus is Lord over all the earth and will one day rule it literally and physically (Rev. 11:15).

9. If you reject Jesus and His absolute claims over your life you are eternally lost and have no other way to approach God (Mk. 8:38; Heb. 10:26–31).

10. Jesus is God's only human representative. He has no "vice-president" living or dead. He lives and reigns forever over all who willingly bow the knee and obey Him as Lord (1 Tim. 2:5).

11. He will lavishly reward everyone who serves Him sacrificially and in sincerity (Matt. 10:42; 16:25–28).

Accepting all of this and living each day accordingly is what we mean by confessing: "Jesus is Lord!" This confession is required of everyone who wants to be his disciple. Christ will not be Savior if he cannot be Lord of all.

## Life Application:
### *Do I Believe This or Not?*

The claims of Jesus must either be accepted or rejected altogether. It is simply impossible to work him into any other system alongside Buddha, Mohammed or any other religious figure. He was either a liar, a lunatic, or he is the Lord. You have to decide what you believe and know why.

Jesus cautioned that we must count the cost carefully and be fully assured in our deepest heart, because those who follow Him will be persecuted and face many trials before they see his face in glory. Accepting Him, however, immediately ushers us into sweet communion and fellowship with the One we were created to love. There is no deeper peace. That's what Jesus promised.

### *I Need Some Help on This, God!*
The Bible promises that God will himself, give evidence to those who seek to know the truth about Jesus.

*Hebrews 2:1–4*: God himself will testify to it by signs, wonders and various miracles, and gifts of the Holy Spirit distributed according to his will. (i.e., God will choose the way).

Sometimes this evidence is a healing, a vision, a dream or an amazing circumstance. Other times it is a tangible sense of His presence, or a deep settled conviction arising from studying the Bible, verifying that what Jesus said about himself is truth. God will choose the exact means, but He has promised to make it real to us.

Christ's own disciples didn't believe it until they saw him alive again after his death on the cross. He spent 40 days with them so they could be certain it wasn't group hysteria or a dream. His followers confidently faced their individual violent deaths over the next 50 years. No amount of torture could dissuade them. They had nothing to gain by lying about the resurrection. Their insistence on it brought them only banishment from their families and poverty. But they knew what they knew. They knew it was true and it changed their lives forever.

### Crossing Over in Faith

It is good to carefully consider the claims of Jesus before accepting Him as Lord, but at some point you just have to make your choice. If you decide for Christ it must become publicly known. There are no "closet Christians." That final moment is a leap, not so much of faith, but of laying our own reputations for self-sufficiency and becoming a humble, broken servant of God. (Read Lk. 9:26; Ro. 10:9 and Heb. 2:13–15)

### Action Steps:

– Enter into a time of honest dialogue with God and the Bible this week. This is a crucial time in your journey of faith. You need to settle forever the question of just who Jesus is.

– In all sincerity, ask God to make you know for certain if the claims of Jesus are true.

– If you decide that you believe in Him, tell Him so and tell someone else also. The proper title for a follower of Jesus Christ is "disciple." A disciple is one who places himself under a master to learn and follow his ways. Begin reading the teachings of Jesus in Matthew, Mark, Luke or John and determine to obey them (Read John 14 on this).

## *Pathways 4: The Deal*

### Approach:
*Listen to this testimony from a young man:* "You don't have to do anything except to just believe and pray this short prayer and you will be saved forever." The man sounded like a TV salesman. Let me get this straight. I get everything, forgiveness, restoration with God, eternal life, promises of divine guidance, healing, provision, etc., and I risk nothing, do nothing, lose nothing, pay nothing? It sounded cheap and empty to me. I prayed, but somehow I knew that something wasn't right about what he said."

*Q: What do you think about this evangelistic message? What is the evangelist trying to get across? Has he missed anything else that the Bible says about God's offer of salvation through Jesus?*

### Bible Exploration:
**Truth 1:** The only reason I am forgiven, made acceptable and blessed is Jesus.

*2 Timothy 1:9–10* There is absolutely nothing I can do to erase my guilt and make myself acceptable to God apart from the perfect sacrifice of Jesus.

**Truth 2:** Jesus paid for it all. Everything is mine by God's grace (unmerited favor) Alone.

*Ephesians 2:8–13* (Please read carefully noting the key words)

**Truth 3:** Salvation through Jesus is available to everyone no matter how good or bad they have been.

*John 3:16–17* "For God so loved the world that he gave his one and only Son, that whoever believes in him shall not perish but have eternal life. For God did not send his Son into the world to condemn the world, but to save the world through him." (Read also 2 Pet. 3:9)

**Truth 4:** To access this priceless gift of grace I must demonstrate the sincerity of my surrender from self-willed living.

While salvation is a gift from God, purchased entirely by Jesus, it is not cheaply and carelessly thrown about. Jesus paid for everyone's salvation, yet everyone will not be saved unless they respond to the offer with integrity. (Read James 4:10)

### The Conditions on the Offer of Salvation are:

**1.** *Confession:* Confession means "agreeing with God's accurate judgment. "We will not be forgiven unless we freely admit the truth of our own guilt and agree with God about our utter helplessness to save ourselves by our own merits. (Read Numbers 5:6–7; Acts 19:18)

It is hard to really see the truth about ourselves because we tend to justify everything we do to avoid guilt. It is good to pray for "godly sorrow," or brokenness. Our hard, stubborn hearts must yield and bow in true sorrow and contrition at the state of our lives before we can really enter into a full release from the deep-seated power of evil with us. Whatever level of sin we have entered into, it was without excuse. God has only done good to us, yet universally and individually we resist His ways and standards. God demands that we admit our guilt to Him and to each other.

*Read James 5:16:* Learning to tell the truth about our lives is a precondition to receiving healing for our brokenness. Without a willingness to become a truth-teller, we will remain hypocrites (those who pretend to be better than they are, carefully covering their faults to find approval from others rather than from God).

*Q: Why do you think God requires us to admit that we are wrong and guilty before He will forgive us?*

**2.** *Repentance:* Repentance involves concrete actions and practical steps by which we demonstrate our full intention to break away from the life of sin. We do this by God's power that enables us day by day. (Read Matt. 3:2, 8, 11; Mk. 6:12)

One act of repentance is the duty to forgive those who have wronged you in any way, accepting the fact that you have wronged God even worse. Since He has forgiven you, you can now surely give the gift of forgiveness to others.

*Q:* (Read Matt. 18:21–35) *Why do you think God requires us to forgive others before He will forgive us?*

Restitution (restoration) is another work of repentance. It means that we pay back what we stole or make amends as fully as we can, for whatever pain and damage we have caused others by our sin.

*Q:* (Read Lk. 19:8–9) *How did Jesus know Zacchaeus was sincere about leaving his corrupt life?*

*More than words:* If we are not willing to forgive, ask for forgiveness or make restitution, our talk of accepting Christ as Lord is only talk. It's not real until our actions back up our words. Faith means, "acting on the basis of my convictions."

*1 John 3:18 (NIV)* Dear Children, let us not love with words or tongue but with actions and in truth. Read James 2:14–18 also.

*Q: How does true faith require more than mental agreement to statement of faith? If mental agreement with the Bible's doctrines was all that faith required, who would also be saved?* (James 2:19)

**3.** *Obedience:* We cannot receive the new life in Christ and continue to live in sin.

– *1 John 1:6* If we claim to have fellowship with him yet walk in the darkness, we lie and do not live by the truth.

– *1 John 1:7* But if we walk in the light, as he is in the light, we have fellowship with one another, and the blood of Jesus, his Son, purifies us from all sin.

*Q: What is the only real proof that a person loves God?*

*Q: They do what the Lord commands* (Read Jn. 14:15, 21, 23, 24)

### Power to Obey:

God will give us the power to obey his good laws which he will write in our hearts, on a renewed conscience that knows His will. When we fail to obey what our hearts tells us to do, we do not quit. We confess, repent and determine to learn from our mistake next time so that we can claim the victory Christ has won for us over the power of sin.

*Romans 6:14* For sin shall not be your master, because you are not under law, but under grace

*Romans 6:18* You have been set free from sin and have become slaves to righteousness

*Not just Once:* Confession, repentance, obedience (the big three) are not one-time events. They must become my lifelong patterns of living with God and others. In this way our pattern of life is purified and we can begin to function as beacons that draw others to the truth about Christ.

*Let's Hear It Again:* Actions of Faith Are Required: Some refuse to do all of this. They enjoy the insufficient message of the evangelist in our introduction. They trust in a cheap grace that allows them to remain as they are and have a mental excuse to hope for God's blessing now and for heaven when they die. Many of these will be rudely awakened on the Day of Judgment.

(Read Matt. 7:21–29 and 25:34–46)

*Q: What evidence was missing in their confessed loyalty and dedication to Jesus?*

### Life Application:
Acting in Faith

*Q: Have you ever had to make a painful apology?*

*Q: What concrete actions of confession, repentance or obedience is God calling you into now?*

### Action Steps:
– *Take a fearless moral inventory:* sit in a quiet place with a blank piece of paper and pen handy. Ask God to show you the truth about your sins. List everything He shows you about your own actions in the past. Confess freely everything He shows you. Justify and excuse nothing.

– *Your turn to act:* Ask God to show you who you have to apologize to, who you must forgive and to whom you must make restitution. Pray for conviction and courage so that you will be a true and obedient disciple of Jesus.

– Determine this week to be more transparent, even about your faults, flaws and sins.

**Prayer:** If you or someone you know would like to accept Jesus as Lord the following prayer is a helpful guide. After praying it, be sure to pray conversationally with words of your own choosing.

"Father God, I feel you drawing me to yourself. I believe that you have shown me with certainty that Jesus is your Son and that He was sacrificed for my sins. I confess that I am a sinner. I turn my back on my old life and I turn my heart to you. I ask that Christ's blood be applied to cancel the record of my sins and I believe that through his death I am now made clean before you and that I am forever adopted as your child. Thank you for this amazing sacrifice. It shows me how valuable I am to you. Thank you for loving me much and please show me how to live in a way that pleases you. I want you to use me to help others know you too. I pray this prayer in the name of Jesus. Amen."

**Memory Verse:** *Acts 4:12 (NIV)* "Salvation is found in no one else, for there is no other name under heaven given to men by which we must be saved."

## Pathways 5: The Holy Spirit and Our New Nature in Christ

### Approach:

*Q: What changes has God been working inside you since you began the Pathway Studies? Q: Complete this sentence: I become weakened in my battle against sin when . . .*

### Bible Exploration:

Becoming a true child of God is a supernatural experience of being changed in our inmost nature and of having the character and power of God imparted to us. This process of rebirth has many dimensions. We receive:

### A new birth

In John, chapter three, Jesus is speaking to a prominent lawyer about his need to surrender everything and find a new life in God. The man, Nicodemus, hesitated, wanting to argue theology. Jesus put his finger on the man's true issue in John 3:8 (NIV) "The wind blows wherever it pleases. You hear its sound, but you cannot tell where it comes from or where it is going. So it is with everyone born of the Spirit."

In other words, once you give your life to God you will lose control of it for your self. (There can't be two bosses.) That was why Nicodemus was hesitating.

*Q: Are you afraid of what God might do if you really gave him complete control? What's the worst thing you think He could ask you to do for Him?*

*Q: Why is it important for us to let the old life die rather than putting bandages on it?*

### A new heart

In order to follow God we need a new inner guidance system since our old one led us into sin and the self-willed life. God has promised just such a gift:

*Ezekiel 36:26 (NIV)* "I will give you a new heart and put a new spirit in you; I will remove from you, your heart of stone and give you a heart of flesh." (i.e., a soft heart)

*Q: Describe what a stony heart would be like? How would a hard, stubborn heart manifest itself in our relationships with God and others?*

### A new inner guide
We can't trust our old conscience

The weakness of the conscience is that it can be desensitized. If you do the same wrong thing over and over, you won't feel bad about it after a while. The next verse describes people who have continually violated their consciences:

*1 Timothy 4:2 (NIV)* "Such teachings come through hypocritical liars, whose consciences have been seared. "

So, in fact that you don't feel bad about doing something doesn't mean that it isn't wrong. God wants you to follow Him perfectly so He will put His own Holy Spirit inside our bodies. Those who receive the "new birth" Jesus promised will receive internal guidance from the Holy Spirit. John 14–15 describes this new reliable Inner Guide.

### The Work of the Holy Spirit
– He convicts us of our sin so that we turn to God for salvation

– He brings us to life as new spiritual creatures. We start life over. (Jn. 3:3–6; 2 Cor. 5:17)

– He makes us to feel accepted into God's family (Ro. 8:16)

– He teaches us (Jn. 14:26)

– He guides us in our decisions (Ro. 8:14)

– He helps us avoid sin (Gal. 5:16)

– He develops the personal character of God in us (Gal. 5:22f)

– He helps us in prayer (Ro. 8:26)

– He opens our understanding about the word of God (1 Cor. 2:9–10)

– He teaches us to worship (Eph. 5:18–19)

These are automatic works of the Spirit when we truly receive the new birth experience after confessing our sins and accepting Jesus as our new Lord and authority. You may not "feel" anything initially, but if the Holy Spirit is living within you will certainly begin to notice major changes in your lifestyle and your inner disposition.

*Q: If you have been born again, what changes have you noticed? Testify about this to give God praise.*

### New Abilities
### Baptism into the Spirit

Aside from the automatic work of the Spirit as He moves in and takes control, there is an additional work which empowers the believer supernaturally for the works of service God intends them to do. In this regard the Holy Spirit:

– Gives us power and boldness to witness for Jesus (Acts 1:8)

– He introduces us to the supernatural realm (1 Cor. 12:4, 8–10)

– He imparts supernatural abilities from God to aid us in the ministry whenever needed (1 Cor. 12)

– He gives us a prayer language (Acts 2:4–13, 17–21, 38–39) by which our deepest communication with God can bypass the bottleneck of our minds. (Ro. 8:26–27; 1 Cor. 14:14)

– He gives us the power to heal the sick and cast out demons that are tormenting people (Matt. 18:8; Mk. 16:16–17)

– The baptism of the Holy Spirit is an experience, not just a doctrine. In the Bible it is always accompanied by some kind of unusual supernatural visitation, most notably the release of the gift of tongues in the believer. Sometimes this happens at the moment of salvation. Often, however, it is a second work after receiving Christ as Lord. However, it comes to you, Peter declared that it is for you and your children (Acts 2:39). You need to seek earnestly the release of these gifts within you. They are a necessary part of God's work in and through you (1 Cor. 14:1).

### A New Mission in Life

Jesus came into this world with a divine purpose

*Q: What was it? (Lk. 19:10)*

Our lives have a divine purpose also *(Read 2 Cor. 5:18–20).*

Q: *What is our mission? We take up the unfinished work of Jesus: seeking and saving the lost. We become his ambassadors to the lost. God will empower and guide us, because the ministry of reconciliation is now our life's work.*

**Life Application:**
Q: *Which of the works of the Holy Spirit do you need most right now?*

Q: *Have you become conscious of God's presence lately? Are you growing to experience entering into God's presence in worship and prayer?*

**Action Steps:**
– Ask God to send the Holy Spirit to live in within you in all His power and glory (write the prayer).

– Every day this week, upon waking, say, "Good Morning Holy Spirit! I look forward to your leadership today!" Then consciously make the effort to be aware of His leading before you speak, act or make a choice.

– List five friends who need to meet Christ. Pray for them daily. Look for a chance to speak with them about this. Trust the Holy Spirit to teach you what to say.

**Memory Verse:** *Acts 2:38 (NIV)* Peter replied, "Repent and be baptized, every one of you, in the name of Jesus Christ for the forgiveness of your sins. And you will receive the gift of the Holy Spirit."

# Letters

Here is a sample of letters we receive from people who are reading "I want to bear Fruit!" and are applying its four-step method of relational evangelism as they go through their days. We have heard testimonies from Africa, Russia, the Middle East, Europe, Asia and the US. Send us your stories too at info@quinley.com.

Dear Chuck,

Words cannot really express the impact that your book has had on my life. The first time I got through reading it I fell on my face before God and was there for about 2 hrs, the anointing was so heavy and I was so broken. I then began to pray the four step commitment every day and at first nothing happened but now I'm finding opportunities everywhere and have prayed with several people on the spot. I'm yet looking forward to greater harvest. Recently we started a lunch hour fellowship at work and I would like to share your book with them. How can I obtain more copies of your book? I need about 5 more copies for now and it's not available in our local bookstores. My copy was given to me by a friend and I do not want to part with it.

Thanks for writing this book

C (Nairobi)

Dear Chuck& Sherry,

Your book on bearing fruit continues to bless me. Yesterday I was able to lead one of my patients to the lord using the principles in your book. It was real neat cause I went to see her in the nursing home and she was so depressed so I got a chair and listened to her story then I shared my testimony and then we prayed and she surrendered her life to the lord. We also prayed about the things that were making her depressed, one of which was having no money. I was able to give her a little money for Christmas, you should have seen her face light up. I tell you I felt so fulfilled, and she had an instantaneous answer to her prayer.

Also we are continuing to study your book at our Lunch-hour bible study at work. We are now on chapter 10 and I believe it is impacting everyone's life.

Dear Chuck,

I'm writing you from Cairo, Egypt, where my husband and I have been living & working for many years.

On his last trip to the States, he came back with your book "I want to bear fruit!". Indeed! We both feel this all the time, and recently I have been concerned about this as I've felt I'm just so busy trying to finish many projects before returning to our home country for 6 months in July.

I wanted to: 1. Encourage you and thank you, 2. Share a brief testimony, and 3. Ask permission to make summary notes of points from the book; and perhaps to even have it translated to Arabic here (if a need is revealed).

So... Firstly: I want to thank you and encourage you for you book. You've clearly "got the message" and have been able to present it clearly. There are so many similarities to what I've realized/learned/noticed.

It is natural, it is freeing, and it is God's plan. Your introductory chapters (before the 4 points) were extremely good at setting the theme, and getting the principles and reasons why clearly laid out. Inspiring - each chapter. I did indeed pray as you suggested.

Secondly, I had a brief working retreat for 2 nights outside of Cairo (this place is just too much at times), and I
took public transport to get there - walk, metro, walk,
bus. Well, I prayed before setting out - and reminded
myself again once on the metro. I felt my own tension..
and prayed. Immediately I felt God's heart for a man di-
agonally opposite me - who was clearly nervous and fid-
gety. I was open to speak to the man if that's what God
wanted, but it didn't happen - but I felt to pray about
some specific things, and asked for Calm to come over
the man and for God to reveal himself in the man's sleep
(this happens here!). I noticed a difference in the man by
the end of the 20 minute ride.

I also noticed that the tension in my own face had left
and I had a peaceful disposition and slight smile. So
THAT was fantastic. Prayed that God would enable us
to meet again if His will – extremely unlikely in this city
of 20 million, but, hey! (By the way my own testimony is
all about "coincidences -just too many to be coinci-
dence!" So it was great to hear your comments about
that.)

Then I walked to a main bus station. God was just amazingly at work in many special relationship ways with
people I met (I can detail more if interested). But it was
really special and unusual and I knew God was in it.
Amazing conversations with a young boy, who I called
'my friend' to some others, and whom I bought a sandwich for. And with others at the sandwich bar whom I
spoke with; I had the 'scraps' of chicken on the grill made
into an extra small sandwich, and then I offered it to the
man sitting beside me. At the end, they said "You are really generous people" (in hindsight, I wished I'd said
some things to that but hey..).

And lastly on the final leg (bus), I prayed that I'd sit beside the one God wanted. I sat down, then had to move...

Have to? Yup. Sat in a seat on my ticket. A guy came to sit beside me (I had my bag on my lap - crowded). Have to? Yup. OK. Well, ended up talking about lots of things and laughed... and later as the conductor checked my ticket, the man beside me noted that I was in the wrong seat! So I told him how I'd prayed that God seat me beside someone He wanted me to speak to - and 'you were it'! Neat.

Then I shared all that and especially about the lessons I learned from your book with my Egyptian host (at the retreat). He was just so encouraged - he said "you always teach me so many things". No - it's from this great book!

Later at work, I shared it too. The man is involved in many groups... and he begged me to find the time to summarize points. (I'd thought before that, that this would be an excellent book to have translated and available for here - especially freeing is the "share as you're led along the normal business of your day"!).

So, thirdly, is my request for permission for me to summarize some points and give it to him (might be easier to photocopy some pages and highlight things). Frankly, there were just too many things I highlighted to make it a brief summary! I know that I could normally just make my own notes and give him a copy. But felt to ask your permission.

So, again, I thank you. I apology for the rambling letter! Don't we all hate long e-mails?! But, hey, YOU asked for it...

Your sis in Christ,

J.   (Cairo, Egypt)

PS.  Please use 'discretion' in writing to me here.

# Order Form

Please mail this form to the following address:

Mt. Paran Bookstore
2055 Mt Paran Rd
Atlanta, GA 30340

Or email the order to us at info@quinley.com

The book is available in Russian and Japanese as well.

Thanks,

Chuck & Sherry Quinley

Number of books ordered: _____

Order to be Shipped to:

Name: _____

Address: _____

_____

City: _____

State: _____

Postal Code: _____

Country (if outside the US): _____

*Contact fax or email:

_____

*Order cannot be completed without this information to verify payment and shipping details

Check us out on the Pathway Press website at:
www.pathwaybookstore.com